MICH.

INT 75

Alexandria Bay

INT 87 White River Jct.
Brattle-boro Pitts-field N.Y. MASS.

INT 89 Nashua N.H. Lowell
cord Portsmo

INT 81

Syra-cuse Utica

INT 90

Boston

Ro-chester

Niagara Falls

Albany

INT 87 Spring-field

INT 84 Hart-ford

Worcester MASS.

INT 91

Providen

New Bedfor

INT 90N Buffalo

Port Huron

and pids Lan-sing

INT 77

Erie

INT 90

N.Y. PA.

N.Y.

Scranton

INT 84

Danbury

New Haven

INT 95

INT 95E

amazoo INT 94

Detroit Conneaut

INT 92

MICH.

Cleveland INT 80

Nor-walk

OHIO PA.

INT 79

INT 80

INT 81S

Easton

Allentown

Harris-burg

New York
Jersey City
Newark
Elizabeth

INT 80

INT 78

Trenton

art

Toledo

Fort Wayne

INT 75

Akron Canton

INT 71

Youngstown

Pittsburgh

INT 80S

Read-ing

INT 80S

INT 83

Philadelphia

Wilmington

9

INT 70

Wheel-ing

PA.
W. VA.

Hagerstown

INT 70S

Strasburg

PA.
Fred-erick

MD.

Baltimore

MD.

DEL.

Indian-apolis

OHIO

Columbus

INT 77

INT 70

INT 70N

D.C.

MD.

Washington DEL.
MD.

Dayton

INT 74

Cincinnati

OHIO

Charles-ton

OHIO
KY.

W. VA.
VA.

INT 66

VA.

Staunton

INT 81

INT 95

55

INT 71

Frank-fort

Lexington

KY.

INT 64

Lexing-ton

INT 64

Richmond

Newport News

Norfolk

W. VA.
VA.

Peters-burg

VA.
N.C.

INT 77

Greens-boro

INT 85

INT 75

KY.
TENN.

INT 40

Knox-ville

INT 81

Winston-Salem

Statesville

INT 40

Durham

Smithfield

Fayetteville

Chatta-nooga

4

TENN.
N.C.

Asheville

INT 26

Charlotte

N.C.
S.C.

N.C.
S.C.

GA.

Greenville

Spartan-burg

INT 20

Florence

INT 95

INT 59

INT 75

INT 85

GA.

Columbia

S.C.

GA.

Summerton

INT 26

Charleston

Atlanta

Augusta

INT 20

La Grange

Macon

INT 16

Savannah

INT 85

GA.
ALA.

Montgomery

INT 75

INT 95

THE YOUNG ADULT ADAPTATION

OVERGROUND RAILROAD

The *Green Book* and the Roots
of Black Travel in America

CANDACY TAYLOR

Amulet Books ★ New York

Map details on endpapers and chapter openers:
National system of interstate and defense highways, published June 1958
by the American Automobile Association. Library of Congress.

Cataloging-in-Publication Data has been applied for and
may be obtained from the Library of Congress.

ISBN 978-1-4197-4949-0

Text copyright © 2022 Candacy Taylor
Edited by Howard W. Reeves
Book design by Sara Corbett

Published in 2022 by Amulet Books, an imprint of ABRAMS.

Printed and bound in China
10 9 8 7 6 5 4 3 2 1

Amulet Books are available at special discounts when
purchased in quantity for premiums and promotions as well as fundraising or
educational use. Special editions can also be created to specification.
For details, contact specialsales@abramsbooks.com or the address below.

ABRAMS The Art of Books
195 Broadway, New York, NY 10007
abramsbooks.com

FOR MOM

CONTENTS

ARE WE THERE YET?

"**D**on't you dare say a word."

Ron was sitting in the back seat as his father pulled the car to a stop at the side of the road. His father had told him to be quiet before, but this was the first time Ron felt the words sink to the pit of his stomach. Moments later, the sheriff stood over the expensive 1953 Chevy sedan.

"Where did you get this vehicle? What are you doing here? And who are these people with you?" the sheriff asked.

Ron at age seven

Ron's father answered, "It's my employer's car."

He pointed to his wife, sitting upright and expressionless in the passenger seat. He pretended that she wasn't his wife and said, "This is my employer's maid, and that is her son in the back. I'm taking them home."

The sheriff took a long, hard look at Ron's mother and then angled his eyes to the back seat. Ron sat tight-lipped, too afraid to turn his head or even take a breath.

"Where's your hat?" the sheriff barked at Ron's dad.

"Hanging up right behind me in the back seat, Officer."

The sheriff waved. "All right. Move on."

As they drove north across the Tennessee border, a sad, eerie silence hung in the air. The jovial conversation they were having right before the sheriff pulled them over had stopped dead. And although there was no discussion about what had just happened, the gravity of the situation was clear. Ron watched Daddy and Mama

Green Book cover, Fall 1956

exchange knowing glances and then turned his head to look at the unassuming black cap that had been hanging next to him in the back seat ever since he could remember. It wasn't until that moment that he realized why he had never seen his father wearing it. Mama wasn't a maid, and Daddy wasn't a driver. He had a good job with the railroad, and this was their family car. Until that day, Ron never paid attention to that cap, but now he realized that it wasn't just any hat. It was a chauffeur's hat. A ruse, a prop—a lifesaver.

This was during the Jim Crow era—from the late nineteenth century until the mid-twentieth—when state and local laws enforced racial segregation in the Southern states, although it was prevalent throughout the country. The chauffeur's hat was the perfect cover for every middle-class Black man pulled over and harassed by the police. If Ron's father had told the sheriff the truth— that he was driving his own car and that they were a family on vacation— the sheriff wouldn't have believed him. He would have assumed the car was stolen. In the event that the sheriff did believe it was Ron's father's car, the rage and jealousy he might have felt at the thought of a Black man owning a nicer car than a police officer might have triggered a beating, torture, or even murder. From that day on, Ron noticed these hats strategically placed, like unarmed weapons, in the back seat of nearly every Black man's car.

Standing in the kitchen, more than fifty years later, I listened to Ron's story, stone-faced.

"Everybody had one," he said, referring to the chauffeur's cap. "And you always kept it in the car."

Ron Burford was my stepfather. I had known this man for more than thirty years, but this was the first time he had told me anything about the pain of growing up in the Jim Crow South. It's not that he was a quiet man; Ron loved to talk. He could talk for hours. My mom and my sister and I would try to scoot out of the kitchen before he started in on another one of his long Southern yarns, ones that we had heard before. But it wasn't until I started the Green Book Project that he shared these stories with me.

Picnic Group, Highland Beach, Maryland, 1931

I first saw a copy of *The Negro Motorist Green Book* in 2014, tucked away under glass at the Autry Museum of the American West, in Los Angeles. It was a travel guide that was published for Black people during the Jim Crow era. Listings in the *Green Book* blanketed the entire United States, and later editions included Canada, the Virgin Islands, Europe, and Africa. The guide was distributed by mail order, sold by Black-owned businesses, and made available through a savvy media campaign led by Esso gas stations (which operate as ExxonMobil today). It was successful due to word of mouth but also as a result of an ambitious grassroots operation of a national network of mailmen led by the guide's creator, and fellow postal worker, Victor Hugo Green. This multipronged marketing strategy was so effective that by 1962, the *Green Book* had a circulation of nearly two million readers.

I'd never known such a thing existed. Right after leaving the Autry, I called my parents in Columbus, Ohio, and asked Ron if he had ever used the *Green Book*.

He said, "I'm not sure; probably. There were a few Black guides back then."

He was right. I discovered there were about a dozen other Black travel guides, but the *Green Book* was in print for the longest period of time and had the widest readership. Victor Hugo Green, a man with a seventh-grade education, published the first *Green Book* in Harlem in 1936, and he worked on it until his death in 1960. His wife, Alma, took up the mantle and kept the *Green Book* going until 1962. What never wavered throughout the life of the *Green Book* was the courage and security it afforded Black people so they could pack up their cars and go.

The *Green Book* was published during a time when car travel symbolized freedom in America: It was affordable to many people and allowed travel from one coast to the other. But since racial segregation was in full force throughout the country, the open road wasn't open to all. Getting to safe accommodations could be a dangerous, life-threatening proposition. Not only did Black motorists navigate a country with thousands of "sundown towns," all-white communities that banned Black people from entering the city limits after dark, but they also couldn't eat, sleep, or buy gasoline at many white-owned businesses. Even Coca-Cola vending machines had "white customers only" printed on them. To avoid the humiliation of being denied basic services, many Black motorists were forced to travel with ice coolers, bedding, portable toilets, and full gas cans.

When Black motorists picked up a copy of the *Green Book*, they were greeted by the words "Just What You Have Been Looking For!! NOW WE CAN TRAVEL WITHOUT EMBARRASSMENT." The businesses listed in it were critical sources of refuge along lonely stretches of America's perilously empty roads. Given the violence that Black travelers encountered on the road, the *Green Book* was an ingenious solution to a horrific problem.

Just What You Have Been Looking For!!

By 1930, Blacks in the United States owned approximately 70,000 small businesses, and over the *Green Book*'s nearly thirty-year reign, it listed more than 9,500 of these, including hotels, restaurants, gas stations, department stores, tailors, nightclubs, drugstores, hair salons, funeral homes, real estate offices, and even a dude ranch—a ranch converted into a vacation resort.

More than 80 percent of the listings were clustered in traditional African American neighborhoods such as Harlem, South Central Los Angeles, and Bronzeville in Chicago. The majority were Black-owned, but there were also Black-friendly white-owned establishments, such as Macy's, Brooks Brothers, the Drake Hotel in Chicago, the Hotel Bel-Air in Los Angeles, and even Disneyland.

AUdubon 3-9016

AUTO ★ REPAIRS
HELP!!

J. JONES
GENERAL AUTO REPAIRS
IGNITION SPECIALIST
BRAKES RELINED

120 West 145th St.   New York City

— DILLARD'S ENTERPRISES —
We offer complete service for the tourist . . .

- **A Tourist Home**
  Clean, Comfortable
  with Showers
- **A Restaurant**
  Offering the best in
  home cooked foods
- **A Beauty Salon &
  Barber Shop**
  For the tourist
  convenience

Stop with us on your trip through historic Virginia
Mr. and Mrs. Fred Dillard, Props.

802 W. Fayette   Martinsville, Va.

KEEP THIS GUIDE WITH YOU

LA FONTAINE SERVICE

DYEING

CLEANING

TAILORING

VALET

Store No. 1
470 CONVENT AVE.
EDgecombe 4-1365

Store No. 2
764 ST. NICHOLAS AVE.
AUdubon 3-7976

Katherine Fontaine   Elliott Fontaine
We Call and Deliver Anywhere

Phone: AU. 3-0671

THE TALK OF THE TOWN WHEN IN NEW YORK

LITTLE ALPHA SERVICE

84 West 120th St.   200 WEST 136th St.
Cor Lenox Ave.   Cor. 7th Ave.

ONE OF NEW YORK'S PIONEER CLEANERS, WHERE SERVICE IS JUST
A SMILE.

6-8 HOUR SERVICE—R. E. EUBANKS, MGR.

Opposite page: *Green Book*, 1948. This page, top: auto repair advertisement from
the *Green Book*, 1938; bottom right: tailor advertisement from the *Green Book*,
1937; bottom left: Dillard's Enterprises advertisement from the *Green Book*, 1961.

Intrigued by the *Green Book*, I wondered how many establishments still existed. So I hit the road scouting *Green Book* listings; I drove nearly forty thousand miles on America's two-lane highways, across acres of wide-open plains and deserts, over mountains, and along coastlines. I also passed miles of boarded-up buildings in Baltimore, Detroit, Chicago, and Cleveland. After seeing communities decimated by poverty, crime, and destructive government policies, I was bewildered, brokenhearted, and then furious that human beings were living in such inhumane conditions.

On the road I was verbally threatened, chased by dogs, physically lunged at, and nearly physically assaulted. I understood the risks and took things one day at a time. The only moment I really feared for my life was when I was scouting *Green Book* sites on the South Side of Chicago. Fifty-three people had been shot the same weekend I was there. Although I was trained in Model Mugging (a program of self-defense for women), there would be nothing I could do to stop a stray bullet. On the days I was too nervous to get out of my car to pump gas or the times when it was too dangerous to stand on the streets to photograph sites, I would think the whole point of the *Green Book* was to keep Black motorists safe on the road, but it's eighty years later and I can't find a safe place to use the bathroom.

As I crisscrossed the country, the words Victor Green wrote in his introduction to the *Green Book* rang through my mind: "There will be a day sometime in the near future when this guide will not have to be published. That is when we as a race will have equal opportunities and privileges in the United States. It will be a great day for us to suspend this publication[,] for then we can go wherever we please, and without embarrassment. But until that time comes we shall continue to publish this information for your convenience each year."

Despite the overt racism Victor Green must have experienced during his life, when he wrote this introduction, he had reason to be optimistic. Just a few years before he created the *Green Book*, the concept of the American Dream was born. It was defined by James Truslow Adams in 1931 as "a dream of social order in which each man and each woman shall be able to attain to the fullest stature of which they are innately capable, and be recognized by others for what they are, regardless of the fortuitous circumstances of birth or position." It was an ambitious goal, but Americans from all races, no matter their economic or social standing in society, wanted to believe in the American Dream.

Remember, there was no established civil rights movement in the 1930s, no Dr. Martin Luther King Jr., so to be a Black business owner during the Jim Crow era was the highest expression of the American Dream.

I realized I wasn't interested in presenting the *Green Book* as a historic time capsule. I wanted to show it in the context of this country's ongoing struggle with race and social mobility, because the problems Black Americans face today like police brutality, homicide, unfair drug sentencing, and mass incarceration are arguably just as debilitating and deadly as the problems the *Green Book* helped Black people avoid more than eighty years ago.

The *Green Book* deserves special attention now because our past and current policies shape how not just Black people but people of all races and gender identities navigate this country. During my research for this book, I learned so much about America just by getting off the interstate and driving through neighborhoods. Photographing *Green Book* sites gave me a greater understanding of and insight into the guide that I never would have had merely reading it in my office at Harvard University. On the road, I felt the tenor of a bygone era and saw a new cycle of grit and survival along Martin Luther King Jr. Boulevards and in the dilapidated houses on dirt roads across the nation.

Wonderland Liquor, a former *Green Book* site in Baltimore, Maryland, 2016

I found strength and resolve in the *Green Book* buildings that are still standing. *Green Book* sites range from A-frame houses to simple storefronts to Spanish Colonial hotels. Regardless of their stature, these former safe zones are symbols of refuge that redefine sanctuary and the story of race in America. After three years of scouting nearly five thousand *Green Book* sites, I learned that more than 75 percent no longer exist and of those remaining, less than 5 percent are still in business. That is why it was so important for me to document the ones that are left.

In most traditional African American neighborhoods, *Green Book* buildings were destroyed in the name of urban renewal, a federal program that gave cities large grants to rebuild their failing downtowns and other urban neighborhoods. Cities could buy and raze "blighted" areas, often residential neighborhoods, and build new housing as well as pay private developers to create new highways, office buildings, and shopping malls. Many pointed out that the program amounted to "Negro removal" because of the way it destroyed thriving Black communities.

Many of the remaining *Green Book* sites are in ruins, and others have been leveled or radically modified beyond recognition. While traveling, I ran a tight ship, following a mapping system in which I could scout thirty sites a day. Since most of them are gone, there were times when I would drive for days and not find a single one. On the rare occasion when I did find a *Green Book* listing that was still in business, it towered over the sidewalk like a rare and beautiful force of nature. It's incredible that any business would survive up to seventy years. Given that most *Green Book* businesses were owned by Black families, to find one that is still operating was reason enough to celebrate. The sites that are still with us symbolize survival: They endured the times the pendulum of equality swung forward and a wrecking ball swung-back.

Green Book businesses are powerful. They shape the narrative of Black mobility and tell a story that is not all about struggle. These sites of sanctuary symbolize Black ingenuity, resourcefulness, strength, entrepreneurship, and resilience. They carry a cultural memory with them and reveal the untold story of Black travel, offering us a rich opportunity to reexamine America's story of segregation, Black migration, and the rise of the Black leisure traveler.

Chapter 1

THE BUSINESS OF THE *GREEN BOOK*

Victor Green was on a mission to find the best printer he could, so he headed down to 800 Sixth Avenue, near Twenty-Eighth Street, in Manhattan's Flower District. He walked past the trash bins filled with fresh-cut flower rejects, entered the building, and rode the service elevator up to the third floor, where the offices of Gibraltar Printing and Publishing Co. were located. There he met Howard Glener, the seven-year-old son of the print shop's owner.

Victor Hugo Green

CUT RATE PRINTING
It's Foolish to pay MORE!
We do not employ any Salesmen
CUT RATE PRICES
You Save Salesman's Commission
from 25 to 33%

1000 Business Cards $4.00
1000 Envelopes $4.00
1000 Statements $4.00
1000 Lettterheads $5.00
1000 Bill Heads in pad form $6.00
SPECIAL PRICES IN LOTS OF 5,000
Prices are subject to change without notice.
MONEY saved by buying from
us, is MONEY earned—
W H Y   P A Y   M O R E ?
This is YOUR opportunity to order Print-
ing Direct from us. All you are charged
for is Labor and Material.
ALL CASH SALES
Mail Your Order or Call at Factory.
GIBRALTAR
PRINTNG & PUBLISHING CO., INC.
800 Sixth Ave., New York 1, N. Y.
Telephone MUrray Hill 4-1189

Green Book advertisement for
Gibraltar Printing

The grown-up Glener remem-bered seeing Victor Green for the first time: "He was a very tall man, impeccably well dressed. He was wearing a suit, a tie, and a hat." Gibraltar's was a white-owned print shop, and it was the first time Glener had seen a Black man there; in fact, it was unusual to see a Black man in this area of Manhattan at all. Glener said, "I don't know if he would have been served coffee in the local Greek diner down the street." Green was "very distinguished," he remem-bered. "He had a manner about him."

Legend has it that Victor Green got the idea to produce a Black travel guide from watching his Jewish friend use a similar guide for Jewish people to vacation in the "Borscht Belt," an area of resorts in New York State's Catskill Mountains. Green teamed up with a fellow postal worker named George I. Smith to publish the first *Green Book* in 1936. The first edition was small, only ten pages, but it was a mighty weapon in the face of segregation. After two years, Green and Smith parted ways for unknown reasons, but Green's brother, William H. Green, joined Victor and his wife, Alma, in the project, editing the *Green Book* until he died in 1945.

Producing each *Green Book* must have required an enormous amount of time and effort, but Victor Green kept his day job as a full-time letter carrier for the U.S. Post Office, commuting from Harlem to Hackensack, New Jersey, five days a week. The commute, coupled with the labor of delivering mail in snow, ice, wind, and rain, must have been exhausting, but Green kept the job because it was reliable, stable employment. During his career, he was a member of the National Association of Letter Carriers, a predominately white union. There was a Black postal union, the National Alliance of Postal and Federal Employees, but Victor joined the association. Just as Green had forged a relationship with a white-owned printer, this was highly unusual. Still, his charisma must have won the white union members over, as he stayed with the union for forty years.

After his day job, Green worked nights and weekends on his guide. There were at least six other Black travel guides on the market while the *Green Book* was in publication, but none was in print as long as or had the reach and readership of the *Green Book*. He worked hard to make his stand out. In the 1939, 1940, and 1941 editions, a brand identity emerged, and the *Green Book* hit its stride with a consistent cover design, feature articles, and a two-column layout. The 1939 edition included listings for every state except Nevada, New Hampshire, and North Dakota.

The cover for the 1948 *Green Book* features a dapper man wearing a tailored double-breasted coat, a tie, a hat, and two-toned wingtip shoes. His female companion wears the rounded-toe baby doll pumps that had just hit the stores that year. The houses, trees, and one falling leaf in the background place the couple in a nice suburban neighborhood. Both are carrying suitcases and smiling, and decide to look our way in midstride en route to their car, to the left of the frame. This couple was so dynamic that their image became part of the logo Green used in following editions and on his business stationery for years.

The *Green Book*'s longevity and success stemmed from Victor Green's vision, grit, creativity, and stamina. Like most of the other guides, the *Green Book* was distributed by mail order and word of mouth. But it was Green's ingenious idea to enlist an army of letter carriers to comb America's streets for advertisers that made the *Green Book* into one of the most densely packed black-and-white travel guides on the market.

Victor Green's office in Harlem was down the hall from the National Alliance of Postal and Federal Employees, a group of mostly Black union mailmen, so he partnered with them and the National Association of Letter Carriers. They took *Green Book*s with them as

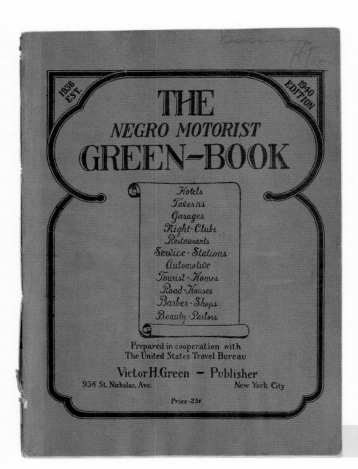

Green Book cover, 1940

they delivered mail, and since the postal service was segregated, they were mostly assigned to work in Black neighborhoods. Many of these postal workers knew the Black business owners and encouraged them to advertise in the *Green Book*. After 1939 the *Green Book*s boasted more than one thousand listings, and nearly ten thousand businesses were advertised over the life of the guide.

Green was determined to make the best product he could. He opened the 1939 edition with a letter announcing that all the businesses listed had been selected "with care" and were the best and most "responsible in their field." For the first couple of editions, Green traveled to personally inspect many of the places listed in the guide, but of course, as it expanded across the eastern United States and then on to the West, there was just too much ground to cover.

To remedy this, he asked readers who visited businesses during their travels to "please mention the *Green Book* . . . ask them to get in touch with us so that we might list their place." He also wrote, "If this guide has proved useful to you on your trips, let us know. If not, tell us also[,] as we appreciate your criticisms and ideas for the improvement of this guide from which you benefit."

By 1948 Green needed help, so he placed ads seeking full- and part-time sales agents to find new businesses to list, inspect properties, and sell subscriptions and advertising space. It was, he assured them, an "excellent opportunity to earn extra money on a commission basis [that] will not interfere with your regular work."

Green also looked for people to submit articles about "Negro motoring conditions, scenic wonders . . . places visited of interest and short stories on one's motoring experience." Two dozen articles were published over the life of the *Green Book*. They included personal trips, but also pieces highlighting automobile culture, airline and railroad travel, and the national parks. Others profiled particular U.S. cities, such as Denver, Los Angeles, Louisville, New Orleans, New York City, San Francisco, and Washington, DC.

The 1939, 1940, and 1941 *Green Book*s were packed to the margins with restaurants, hotels, and a host of other services, all alphabetized by state, city, and type of business. Although collectively it was an impressive list, there were still parts of the country that had few options available. For instance, the *Green Book* listed only four tourist homes in the entire state of Wisconsin. New Mexico and South Dakota listed two tourist homes each, and there were only two hotels offered in Miami.

Green must have found strength from the supporters who stopped in his office to congratulate him, some leaving orders for the next edition. He must have cherished letters such as the one he received from William Smith, a New Jersey resident, who wrote:

> *It is a great pleasure for me to give credit where credit is due. Many of my friends have joined me in admitting that "The Negro Motorist Green Book" is a credit to the Negro Race. It is a book badly needed among our Race since the advance of the motor age. Realizing the only way we knew where and how to reach our pleasure resorts was in a way of speaking, by word of mouth, until the publication of "The Negro Motorist Green Book" . . . We earnestly believe "The Negro*

Motorist Green Book" will mean as much if not more to us as the AAA [American Automobile Association aka Triple A] means to the white race.

The *Green Book* was filling a critical need for Black Americans, which was the key to its success. No official business records from Green's office survive today, so there is no way to know how many copies were sold. Some reports have estimated that approximately fifteen thousand were sold each year, and another estimate has more than two million copies circulated in 1962 alone.

As with most travel guides, it's assumed that the *Green Book* didn't charge businesses to be included but Green did encourage them to purchase ads. Yet he was so committed to helping Black business owners that he offered to promote them even if they didn't pay for advertising. Green encouraged businesses to "drop us a line and send us some of your business cards and other printed matter you may have for distribution and we will endeavor to do our best to boost your business." This also might have helped fill in sections of the *Green Book* covering certain areas of the country with fewer accommodations.

Green continued to work at the post office full time after starting the *Green Book* venture. After retiring from the post office in 1952, he worked full time on the guide until his death in 1960. Although he didn't get rich off the *Green Book*, his reward was much more valuable than money, because for every business he listed, he may have saved a life.

Chapter 2

DRIVING WHILE BLACK

When the first edition of the *Green Book* came out, there were nearly thirty million cars on the road. In January of the following year, Franklin D. Roosevelt was inaugurated into a second term as U.S. president, and many Americans, Black and white, were optimistic about the future. Seven years had passed since the Great Depression, and Black employment was the highest it had been.

Victor Green created his guide in this era of optimism, and the first two

Photographer Zack Brown shooting a dapper man in Harlem, circa 1937

editions were centered on New York City's Harlem, where he and Alma lived. Today, Harlem is the iconic heart of Black culture and identity, but when Victor dreamed up his guide, the neighborhood wasn't yet the Black mecca it eventually became. At the turn of the twentieth century, Harlem was home to a number of recent, white immigrant groups, including Jews, Italians, and Irish. Black people comprised only about 10 percent of the population. Then in the early 1920s there was an influx of African Americans moving into the area, especially from the South, looking for better opportunities for their families. With them came artists, musicians, singers, actors, writers, and others, and suddenly Harlem was the center of a new movement, celebrating African American culture. This period spanned the decade and was called the Harlem Renaissance. The new arrivals increased the Black population to 70 percent by 1930.

The rules for segregated establishments changed from block to block, so Black people didn't know where they would be served. Francis "Doll" Thomas, who started working in Harlem theaters in 1914 and became the film projectionist and the technical director at the Apollo Theater, told author Ted Fox, for his illustrated history *Showtime at the Apollo*:

The Apollo Theater, a former *Green Book* site in Harlem, New York

"There were no blacks on 125th Street. That was all Irish . . . [T]he theater that's now the Apollo, you entered from 126th Street. Up the back stairs. The Alhambra just wouldn't sell [blacks] an orchestra seat. They were either sold out or they'd flatly refuse. Also on 125th Street, Frank's Lunchroom—you couldn't get served in there. Across the street was Childs. You couldn't get served in there. Next door was Loft's Candy Shop. Couldn't get served in there. Right down the street was Fabian's Seafood Shop. Couldn't get served in there."

The Apollo Theater was listed under "Colored Show Houses" in the 1937 *Green Book*. Before it was the Apollo, the building housed the burlesque theater Hurtig and Seamon, which didn't allow Black people to enter through the front door. Once inside, Black ticket holders were banned from general seating and forced to sit in the balcony.

The Apollo opened in 1934, and the following year, Frank Schiffman and Leo Brecher took it over. Schiffman, a white man, told a New York newspaper in 1937, "I'm the largest employer of colored theatrical help in the country"—and he was. For years, the Apollo was one of the only theaters in New York City that hired African Americans, and the majority of its staff was Black. Schiffman's family operated the Apollo until the late 1970s, and they are often credited with integrating 125th Street. Schiffman also helped launch the careers of Ella Fitzgerald, Count Basie, Sarah Vaughan, James Brown, Diana Ross, Marvin Gaye, Aretha Franklin, and Billie Holiday.

The Lafayette was another theater listed under "Colored Show Houses" in the 1937 *Green Book*. (At the time, "colored" referred to Black people.) Frank Schiffman and Leo Brecher helped desegregate the Lafayette so that Black audience members were no longer relegated to the balcony. They were now permitted to sit in the orchestra section. The Lafayette was one of the first theaters in Harlem to change its segregationist policies and became the center for Black dramatic and musical talent.

In 1936 Orson Welles produced William Shakespeare's *Macbeth* at the Lafayette, a version retitled *Voodoo Macbeth* with an all-Black cast and the setting changed from Scotland to an island in the Caribbean. Welles hired local Haitians to perform, and in less than one month, some thirty-four thousand people purchased tickets. It would play to capacity for another month before going on tour.

Crowd outside the Lafayette Theatre in Harlem, New York, at the opening of *Voodoo Macbeth*

While the Lafayette and the Apollo were pushing the boundaries of racial segregation in Harlem, the shifting racial demographics were pushing the neighborhood to its breaking point. In 1935, just one year before Victor Green set in motion the plans for his guide, a riot broke out. On March 19, a rumor

The net paid circulation for February exceeded
Daily --- 1,650,000
Sunday- 2,500,000

DAILY NEWS

Copyright, 1935, by News Syndicate Co., Inc. Reg. U. S. Pat Off.

NEW YORK'S PICTURE NEWSPAPER

Entered as 2nd class matter, Post Office, New York, N. Y.

★★★★ **FINAL**

Vol. 16. No. 229   64 Pages   New York, Wednesday, March 20, 1935*   2 Cents IN CITY LIMITS | 3 CENTS Elsewhere

4,000 RIOT IN HARLEM; ONE KILLED

Story on Page 3

A Bottle Crashed

(NEWS photo by Lewis)

Blood streaming down his face, this victim is lifted to his feet by a policeman,

This Boy Started Riot

(NEWS photo by Meurer; © 1935 by News Syndicate Co., Inc.)

A false report spread by radicals that Lino Rivera, 16, (center)

A Girl Victim

(NEWS photo by Sandhaus)

Wrapped in a beautiful fur coat, Patricia O'Rourke, daughter of

Front page of the *Daily News*, March 20, 1935

spread across Harlem that Lino Rivera, a sixteen-year-old Black Puerto Rican teenager, had been beaten to death for stealing a penknife from the S. H. Kress and Co. five-and-dime store. The beating death never happened, but the rumor incited a full-blown race riot. Someone in the crowd screamed, "The boy is dead in the cellar there, but they won't even let a doctor look at him!" Then a brick flew through Kress's window, and rioters, both Black and white, barreled down 125th Street.

During the riot, white store owners tried to protect their property from frustrated Black looters by posting signs that read COLORED STORE or COLORED EMPLOYEE HERE. But it wasn't only Blacks who were violent; on March 20, 1935, the day the fighting ended, the New York *Daily News* reported that "armed bands of [African-American] and white guerillas . . . roamed through barricaded Harlem . . . assaulting every person of opposite color to cross their paths, setting fires and smashing shop windows after a night of fighting, in a bitter continuation of Harlem's worst race riot in twenty-five years." More than five hundred police descended on Harlem to quell the violence. In the end, an estimated two million dollars in damage was done, hundreds of people were wounded, and three African Americans had died. After the riot, Mayor Fiorello La Guardia commissioned a fourteen-member biracial panel to study the conditions that had led to the riot. It concluded that the riot had been caused by "injustices of discrimination in employment, the aggressions of the police, and racial segregation."

The driving force behind Harlem's racial unrest was the long-standing mistrust of the police by African Americans and white merchants' refusal to hire Black residents, which helped keep the Black unemployment rate double the national average. Neighborhoods throughout America where white merchants profited from Black residents but refused to hire them inspired the "Do Not Buy Where You Cannot Work" campaign. This Depression-era movement born in Chicago in 1929 began when the retail store Woolworth refused to hire Black locals. A massive boycott ensued—Blacks were urged not to spend their money in shops and other businesses owned by white people who refused to hire Black employees. Soon after, demonstrations sprang up in St. Louis; Washington, DC; Los Angeles; and Atlanta.

Women demonstrating for the "Do Not Buy Where You Cannot Work" campaign

The National Association for the Advancement of Colored People (NAACP), the oldest civil rights organization in the United States, became involved, too. In the 1931 issue of the organization's official magazine, *The Crisis*, W. E. B. Du Bois wrote in his editorial "The Negro's Industrial Plight," "If we once make a religion of our determination to spend our meager income so far as possible only in such ways as will bring us employment consideration and opportunity, the possibilities before us are enormous." So when

"We Can Fix Em" advertisement from the *Green Book*, 1937

the *Green Book* came along a few years later, it became the perfect complement to the "Do Not Buy Where You Cannot Work" protests, functioning more like a directory for Black-owned businesses than a traditional travel guide.

The 1937 edition was unusual for a travel guide. Only fifteen pages long, it listed more automobile businesses than travel sites. Eighteen of the twenty ads in the first five pages were Harlem-based mechanics, fender and body workers, ignition specialists, welders, tow service providers, and auto painters. (The two non-auto-related ads were for a radio repair shop and a store specializing in an entirely different sort of wheels: Hollis' Bicycle Store, owned by Harri Hollis, who described himself as a "Colored Pro Bike Champ.")

There was a clear market for car-related businesses in the late thirties because by then, 85 percent of Americans vacationed by car. This helped make the automobile industry one of the leading industries in the world. But even more important, a vehicle provided Black families with the freedom and job opportunities they needed to pull themselves out of the servant class and into a stable middle-class lifestyle.

Automobile clip art from the *Green Book*, 1938

Well-dressed boys pose with a car, reflecting its status as an emblem of success. Easter morning, Southside Chicago, 1941.

The 1938 *Green Book* went far beyond the first two, with listings for nearly 220 businesses in Harlem, and included roadhouses, tourist homes, service stations, barbershops, beauty parlors, dance halls, and nightclubs east of the Mississippi River. But it too was fascinated with the automobile. It contained an article, "The Automobile and What It Has Done for the Negro," by Benj. J. Thomas, the proprietor of the Broadway Auto School. In the article Thomas writes, "In New York City alone, one third of the Mechanical work is being done by Colored men. The automobile has been a special blessing to the Negro . . . 25 years ago, the average young colored man was doing porter work, bell hopping, running an elevator or waiting on table[s], and the average wage at that time was $5 per week." Now Black men in the automotive trade who were earning a solid middle-class wage were becoming a crucial part of burgeoning businesses both employing and serving the Black community.

Although auto industry jobs made it possible for many Black families to afford their own cars, it wasn't easy, as the average price of a new car was $760, and the annual salary for most Black men in the auto industry averaged about $1,500—so the purchase price for a car represented more than half a year's income. Regardless, to many Black Americans, the freedom that came with owning a car was worth the sacrifice. Having a car shielded them from physical harm, humiliation, harassment, and the psychological terror of a segregated America. With a car, Black people had an option other than being corralled into subpar seating on buses, streetcars, trolleys, and trains that were almost guaranteed to be uncomfortable and dirty. W. E. B. Du Bois writes about this in *Darkwater: Voices from Within the Veil*:

> *Did you ever see a "Jim-Crow" waiting-room? . . . there is no heat in winter and no air in summer . . . to buy a ticket is torture; you stand and stand and wait and wait until every white person at the "other window" is waited on . . . The agent browbeats and contradicts you, hurries and confuses the ignorant, gives many persons the wrong change, compels some to purchase their tickets on the train at a higher price, and sends you and me out on the platform, burning with indignation and hatred!*
>
> *The "Jim-Crow" car is up next to the baggage car and engine. It stops out beyond the covering in the rain or sun or dust. Usually there is no step*

to help you climb on and often the car is a smoker cut in two and you must pass through the white smokers or else they pass through your part, with swagger and noise and stares. Your compartment is a half or a quarter or an eighth of the oldest car in service on the road . . . the floor is grimy, and the windows dirty.

Avoiding the discomfort and psychological strain of this segregated travel experience is the reason Black Americans did anything they could to have their own car—and the *Green Book* was the perfect guide to support those fortunate enough to afford one.

When the *Green Book* was first published, there were only a few Black-owned car dealerships in the entire country, and auto financing was a significant hurdle for Black consumers. Even those who had the cash had trouble finding dealerships that would sell to them. In many cases, Black people weren't even allowed on the showroom floor. For instance, in the early 1930s General Motors had an unwritten policy not to sell its Cadillacs to Black motorists because the company felt Black people would undermine its brand. So Black consumers got creative and bought the company's cars secondhand or paid white people to act as "front men" and shop for them. It took a while for GM to catch on. The ruse was discovered when Black motorists began to bring their Cadillacs to dealerships for service. Initially, Cadillac mechanics thought these customers were workers bringing in their employers' cars, but once they realized that Black men owned the cars themselves, they were stunned.

Nicholas Dreystadt, a white Cadillac service manager, urged executives to allow Black people in the showrooms, arguing that this was a missed opportunity for potential profits. He pressured General Motors to advertise to Black consumers, and it worked. By the mid-1930s, these marketing efforts had boosted the company's sales and helped GM recover from the Great Depression, so much so that it named Dreystadt the head of the Cadillac division.

Being Black and finally being able to drive a Cadillac still came with its problems. Journalist George Schuyler wrote that "Blacks who drove expensive cars offended white sensibilities," and some Blacks "kept to older models so as not to give the dangerous impression of being above themselves." Some Black people who could afford a nicer car chose to drive a less expensive one to avoid confrontation.

Victor Green was eager to help his community join the ranks of the motoring public. The auto industry was undergoing a significant change, and it was making headlines. This was an exciting time for auto innovation and technology.

On the first page of the 1937 *Green Book*, Victor Green's introduction called on readers to "get together and make Motoring better." Yet preparation for a road trip required extra work for Black motorists planning to travel through a state with only a few *Green Book* listings. They had to prepare for inconveniences and even atrocities that white motorists never had to consider. Even if there was a Black-friendly motel or tourist home listed, there were no guarantees it would have space available. And there was no way to reserve a spot, as most *Green Book* listings didn't include phone numbers.

Black families therefore would spend weeks preparing to travel America's minor roads. They'd pack sheets and blankets, which doubled as privacy partitions in case they had no choice but to relieve themselves on the side of the road. And because there was no guarantee they would find a restaurant, food was packed in ice and placed in "shoebox lunches." Herbert Sulaiman remembers traveling with his parents as a child. "You had to be prepared," he said. "Traveling in those days meant the women would fix food at night. They'd fill the thermos jugs, you had eggs, fixed ham sandwiches and turkey sandwiches and fried chicken."

Boys leave for orthopedic camp, 1958

Despite the uncertainty of what Black travelers might encounter on the road, the *Green Book* focused on solutions rather than problems. Its tone was never threatening, and there was no mention of the dire consequences of being stranded or denied service. Instead, a lighthearted spirit can be found throughout the 1937 edition, which was printed entirely in green ink.

On page 3 of the 1937 edition, the article "Prepardness" [*sic*] begins with "An Ounce of Prevention is worth more than a Pound of Cure" and outlines the importance of getting a proper tune-up, laying out the procedures for those unfamiliar with car maintenance. The tips are thorough, and the advice is practical and positive. "Be prepared before you start, and more than likely you will have a pleasant and enjoyable trip with no regrets when you return."

Underlying his sound mechanical advice is Green's full awareness that for Black drivers, being stranded wasn't just an inconvenience. Depending on where they were, it could mean life or death. In the late 1930s, the federal Interstate Highway System hadn't been developed yet, so cross-country travel required driving long distances on county roads, and along small-town Main Streets, where Black families were much more vulnerable to run-ins with the local sheriffs.

A huge concern for Black motorists was getting stranded in a "sundown town," an all-white enclave that banned Black people from entering after dark. Thousands of sundown towns were scattered throughout the country. Harvard sociologist James Loewen, in his book *Sundown Towns*, defines a sundown town as a city, town, or village that had nine or fewer Black residents. He also traces towns whose Black populations virtually vanished within twenty-four hours of a mob lynching or riot, usually because they were fleeing angry white mobs.

Loewen writes that sundown towns were largely a northern invention, starting in about 1890 and lasting well into the 1960s. In fact, he found hundreds of sundown towns in Illinois alone. The five states with the most sundown towns were Ohio, Kansas, California, Missouri, and Nebraska. Ironically, Mississippi, a state that became a global symbol of terrorism and white supremacy, had only three sundown towns.

DON'T LET THE SUN SET ON YOU HERE, UNDERSTAND

"Don't Let the Sun Set on You Here, Understand." Printed in the *Norman Transcript* newspaper in Norman, Oklahoma; date unknown.

Most sundown towns made it very clear that Black people were not welcome. Some posted signs. Others, such as Villa Grove, Illinois, and Gardnerville, Nevada, rang a bell at six p.m. that warned Black laborers and domestics to leave.

In response to sundown towns, one Black town turned the tables on white travelers passing through their community. Ellen Sue Blakey, a white woman who grew up in southern Oklahoma with her grandparents, tells a story from her childhood about driving to see her great-aunt and -uncle, who lived about sixty miles away.

On the road was a small Black community, whose structures appeared to be left over from the Dust Bowl . . . At the community's edge was a sign obviously inspired by sundown towns and their signs telling Blacks to basically move on. I'm certain someone there felt a tit-for-tat was fair play. The crude hand-lettered sign on the highway read: WHITE MAN DON'T SHOW YOUR FACE HERE AFTER DARK. *My grandfather took it seriously . . . We always made sure we left my great aunt and uncle's house so that we passed through in daylight hours.*

Nearly all the sundown towns are gone now, but there are still communities hostile to Black people. In the northwestern corner of Arkansas, for example, Harrison, a modern-day Klan town in the Ozarks, is littered with white supremacists. Black residents were run out of Harrison after two race riots, in 1905 and 1909. In 2010, among its 12,943 residents, 96 percent were white.

In addition to food and lodging, Victor Green included sites that celebrated the Black middle class and introduced his readers to the upper-class segments of society they wouldn't normally have been exposed to. For instance, the 1937 edition advertised country clubs and four golf courses, two of which, Saxon Woods in Scarsdale and Sprain Lake in Yonkers, are still in operation in New York State. Even today, in spite of Tiger Woods's dominance of the sport since the turn of the twenty-first century, golf isn't generally associated with African Americans, as either players or spectators, yet Green's inclusion of golf courses indicated otherwise.

The exclusion of Black people from golf courses as anything but caddies was commonplace, but in 1943 it was written directly into the Professional

Golfers Association (PGA) bylaws that only "members of the Caucasian race" were allowed to join. (The clause was finally removed in 1961.) Despite the deliberate segregation of the sport, Black people not only participated in but also have influenced the game of golf for more than a century.

Dr. George Grant, an African American dentist, made the most significant contribution when he designed the first golf tee, in 1899. Before his invention, players had to carry buckets of sand from one hole to another to create makeshift mounds from which to tee off. Grant's design became the standard for tees used for decades.

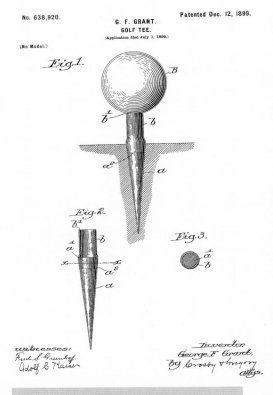

Dr. George Grant's golf tee patent, 1899

Twenty-three years after Grant invented his wooden golf tee, Joseph Bartholomew, a native of New Orleans and a self-taught golfer, became the first African American to design a public golf course, the Metairie Country Club in New Orleans. As a Black man, he was forbidden from playing on this course or any of the several he designed in New Orleans and across the state of Louisiana. If at that time an architect couldn't even walk in the light of day on the golf course he designed, imagine how incredible it must have been to look in the *Green Book* and find golf courses advertised.

Since most recreational facilities were off-limits to Black people, Green's "Let's Go Places" section in the *Green Book*'s 1937 edition was a wonderful feature for those wanting to enjoy fresh air outside the city. Along with golf courses, Green listed New York State parks on Long Island and in Westchester County where African Americans could swim, picnic, and relax on the beach.

Long Island was just thirty miles from Harlem, but for those who didn't have a car, it might as well have been across the Atlantic Ocean. Access to these recreational spaces by poor and marginalized communities both Black and white was limited *by design*. In the span of forty-four years, Robert Moses, president of the New York State Parks Council from 1924 to 1963, along with public agencies, built 13 bridges, 416 miles of highways, and more than 2.5 million acres of parks. Although one of these, Jones Beach, was listed in the *Green Book*, Moses, known as the "master builder" of the twentieth century, was a notorious racist. Historians believe that it was his contempt for poor people of color that motivated him to build the Long Island Expressway overpasses with clearances too low to provide safe passage for the public buses that would have transported them to the beaches and parks he sought to keep white.

Unfortunately, this attitude was shared by people throughout the country. In 1925, just one year after Moses became president of the New York State Parks Council, the *Chicago Tribune* published the following editorial:

> *We should be doing no service to the Negroes if we did not point out that to a very large section of the white population the presence of a Negro, however well behaved, among white bathers is an irritation . . . [T]he Negroes could make a definite contribution to good race relationship by*

remaining away from beaches where their presence is resented.

Most beaches were still segregated twelve years after this *Chicago Tribune* piece was printed, so it must have been exciting for Black readers to see accessible beaches listed in the 1937 *Green Book*. Moses's scheme to shut Blacks out by designing low-clearance overpasses failed because the automobile

Ouida F. Taylor family children at the beach on Martha's Vineyard, 1950s

was their trump card. There were no formal segregation laws on the books in Long Island, so if Black vacationers could get there, no law prevented them from staying. So they packed up their swimsuits, golf clubs, beach towels, and picnic baskets and hit the road.

The South has long been demonized for its history of slavery and, perhaps worse, its defense of it. And as a result the North has been consistently let off the hook, but when bridges and tunnels are designed to corral and control people of color, this is just as bad as, if not worse than, simply posting a Whites Only sign. Presenting the illusion of access and then going to great lengths to employ a hidden, covert system to deny it speaks of an even more insidious racism, and one much harder to fight. For this and so many other reasons, the automobile was powerful for Black physical and social mobility. For Black travelers, armed with the *Green Book*, the vehicle became a formidable tool that pushed the pendulum of equality forward.

Members of the Tuskegee Airmen, a group of primarily African American military pilots and airmen who fought in World War II. Circa 1942.

Chapter 3

THE
FIGHT

World War II (WWII) put an end to leisure travel and temporarily shut down the production of the *Green Book*. Everything changed in the travel industry. President Franklin D. Roosevelt banned pleasure driving, and the rubber shortage was so severe that any American who had more than five tires was required to turn the extras over to the government. Gas rationing required thirty million motorists to display windshield stickers in a three-tiered alphabetical system that assigned how much gas was allotted based on a driver's needs. With the exception of truck drivers, taxi drivers, and physicians who made house calls, most Americans were limited to driving a maximum of eight and a half miles a day.

As a result of the war rations, the *Green Book* was not published between 1942 and 1945, the years the United States was in WWII. But when the war ended, the 1946 and 1947 editions hit the stands with a fresh makeover, a new cover design, and a bold new typeface. The 1946 edition depicts an illustration of a cityscape, and the 1947 cover has a photograph of a simple tree-lined road winding through the Maine countryside. No people—just road, earth, and sky. The photograph was the first to grace the cover of a *Green Book*. From this year forward, each subsequent edition had a photograph or an illustration on the front.

The 1946 and 1947 editions were much larger than the earlier *Green Books*, listing more than three thousand businesses and including every state except North Dakota. They were packed with feature articles. On the cover, the subtitle *A Classified Motorist's & Tourist's Guide Covering the United States* emerged with a new tagline:

*Carry your Green Book with you
. . . you may need it . . .*

Each edition opened with a serious article about Black soldiers returning home from the war and their need for educational services. When African Americans joined to fight in World War II, it was with the intention of achieving a "Double V"—victory over Hitler and the fascism they were fighting abroad and victory over the racism they were fighting at home. Legions of the 1.2 million Black men who enlisted in the U.S. military hoped their service would prove they shared a common purpose with their countrymen and would ultimately humanize them in the eyes of white Americans. Unfortunately, the vast majority of Black men who returned to the States after having fought for freedom came home to a country that still dehumanized them.

Before they left to fight in the war, Black soldiers were often denied services outside the training camps. For instance, Black soldiers stationed at Fort Leonard Wood, near Rolla, Missouri, on Route 66, were shut out of local restaurants and nightclubs, and had to drive eighty miles to Graham's Rib Station, in Springfield, Missouri, for food, fun, and entertainment. Opened in 1932 by an African American couple, James and Zelma Graham, it wasn't listed in the *Green Book*, but the on-site motel, built during the war, offered lodging to Black soldiers, giving them a safe place to stay so they wouldn't have to make the long drive back to their barracks at night.

Graham's Rib Station, Springfield, Missouri, 1930s

Graham's filled some of the needs of Black soldiers, but segregated restaurants and entertainment venues were a minor injustice compared to the military's commitment to keeping Blacks and whites separated even at the nation's blood banks.

Blood donation was a powerful symbol of patriotism, but in 1941 Black Americans were turned away when they tried to donate blood for the cause. The U.S. Army and Navy told the Red Cross they would accept blood only from white donors. The American Medical Association spoke out against the ban, and the director of the Red Cross blood banks resigned in protest, to no avail.

The army was so opposed to integration that it organized segregated redistribution centers, or what the *Chicago Defender*, a prominent Black newspaper, called "Jim Crow Centers," which were developed for returning soldiers to rest before they headed back into combat. Forty-nine hotels were selected throughout the country for white soldiers to swim and play golf, tennis, and shuffleboard. For Black soldiers, the army planned to seize Harlem's Hotel Theresa in New York City and the Pershing Hotel, located on Chicago's South Side, both of which had no spaces for recreational activities.

The Pershing Hotel was the largest Black hotel in Chicago, with two hundred rooms, a beauty shop, a barbershop, a ballroom, and valet service. It was listed in the *Green Book* from 1947 to 1950. The Theresa was Harlem's most glamorous hotel. It was listed in the *Green Book* in 1940 and then in every subsequent edition until 1967.

The army decided to take over these hotels during the height of their popularity. The Theresa, built in 1912–1913, didn't always serve Black people, but by 1947 the three-hundred-room hotel, which was located right down the street from the Apollo Theater, predominantly hosted Black movie stars, musicians, politicians, and athletes. The world heavyweight boxing champ Joe Louis stayed at the Theresa and held his victory parties there while thousands of onlookers gathered outside, hoping to get a glimpse of him. Everyone who was anyone, from jazz player and composer Louis Armstrong and jazz singer Ella Fitzgerald to actresses Dorothy Dandridge and Lena Horne, mingled at the fifty-one-foot J-shaped bar on the street level. Stores on the mezzanine of the Theresa sold fabulous clothes.

In addition to the celebrities, the Theresa was teeming with showgirls, wealthy tourists, socialites, and even gangsters, who played the numbers in the basement. It was a vibrant, exciting hub of Black culture that was called the "social headquarters of Negro America" by *Ebony* magazine. John H. Johnson, the founder of *Ebony* and *Jet,* found the place was such a source of inspiration that he conceived of his magazines while staying at the Theresa.

When the U.S. Army set out to revoke reservations that had been made months in advance and to

Hotel Theresa, Harlem, New York, 1915

evict current guests from the Theresa and the Pershing, the NAACP, the Urban League, the YMCA, and Black newspapers throughout the country vehemently protested, demanding that President Roosevelt reverse the army's decision. On September 30, 1944, four days after the army announced its plans, the *Philadelphia Tribune* published a scathing article, asking, "What kind of people do the officials who run the United States Army think Negroes are anyhow? Do those who control the Army, those who make the rules and regulations, think that Negroes are a bunch of ignorant notwits [*sic*] who possess none of those human attributes which place men above dumb-driven animals? . . . They make rules and regulations which embarrass, insult and humiliate every colored person . . . In other words, the United States Army enforces anti-racial laws in America while seeking to destroy them abroad. This incident proves conclusively that the Army has the power to abolish segregation within its own ranks. The fact that it does not do so proves that those in control do not want to do so; that they consider Negroes as less than men."

Within a month of the publication of the *Philadelphia Tribune* article, the Roosevelt administration pressured the army to revise its plan to segregate returning soldiers. The army relinquished possession of the Theresa and Pershing Hotels and agreed to integrate the redistribution centers. Many Black Americans feared that Black soldiers funneled into southern distribution centers would still be segregated, but at least they knew the northern ones at Lake Placid and Atlantic City would be integrated.

There were so few lodging options for Black travelers at the time that the army saved face by telling the public that was the reason it had reversed its decision to take over the Pershing and Theresa Hotels. In the end, it was a notable victory for the Black resistance and a triumph against the armed forces in the struggle for racial equality.

Pershing Hotel, Chicago, Illinois

Black Americans may have won the battle with the army, but when they returned from Europe, they were still fighting a war for racial equality. These men who had sacrificed life and limb wanted the same respect and admiration their white comrades received when they returned home. But Black soldiers quickly learned that being trained in combat, tactical operations, and weaponry had made them even more feared and hated.

Some white Americans didn't react well to Black soldiers returning from war feeling entitled to fair and equal treatment. This sentiment wasn't new. In 1917, when the United States entered World War I, Senator James K. Vardaman of Mississippi had stated on the Senate floor that allowing Black men to serve in the armed forces was a mistake that would "inevitably lead to disaster," because once you "impress the Negro with the fact that he is defending the flag" and "inflate his untutored soul with military airs," he would demand that "his political rights must be respected."

Once Black soldiers began to return home from WWI, Vardaman's nightmare came true: These veterans expected change. The same repeated itself at the end of WWII. When a Black marine named Timothy Hood snatched down a Jim Crow sign from a streetcar in Bessemer, Alabama, the conductor, William Weeks, shot him five times. Hood, still alive, stumbled off the train and was promptly arrested by the chief of police, G. B. Fant, who delivered a fatal shot to his head. Fant, who claimed Hood had been reaching for a gun in his pocket, was never prosecuted for the murder.

Some white veterans who witnessed the horrible treatment of their Black brethren made valiant attempts to defend their honor. U.S. ambassador to Barbados and Grenada, Theodore Roosevelt Britton served in World War II as one of the first Black marines. He was trained in a segregated camp and remembered a time when one of his fellow soldiers, a Black man who lived in Chicago, was waiting to go home to Louisiana. Britton said, "A tall white marine came up and said, 'Why aren't you getting on the bus?' He said, 'Because they load all the whites first and they take Blacks afterward, but the last two buses were loaded with whites and there was no room.' The white marine said, 'Are you ready to go?' He said, 'Yes.' The white marine called the station manager over. He pulled out his .45 pistol and said, 'The next bus that comes in here I want to see that man in one of those seats or I'm going to see your brains on this floor.' My friend was on the next bus. He was sitting in the back, but he was on his way to Louisiana."

Many Black Americans had joined the marines as a ticket out of the Jim Crow South and to receive an education that would facilitate a better future. The government promised college to World War II veterans with the aid of the GI Bill, which helped cover the costs associated with school or training for career opportunities. This didn't help Black World War II veterans, as most of them were denied entry into white colleges.

Victor Green recognized that this was a problem and consequently featured a list of 106 Black colleges at the beginning of the 1946 and 1947 editions of the *Green Book*. These schools specialized in agriculture, mechanics, social work, theology, and teaching. Today, forty-three of the colleges listed in the *Green Book* are still operating, including Morehouse and Spelman Colleges in Atlanta, Georgia, and Howard University, in Washington, DC.

This comprehensive list of colleges elevated the *Green Book* from a travel guide to a political weapon. An educated Black person was an enduring threat to white supremacy—it's no wonder it had been a crime for Black slaves to learn to read. Still, even with slavery long in the past, educational opportunities continued to elude African Americans. Books were kept out of arm's reach, and Black tax-paying citizens were denied entrance into public, tax-funded libraries. The seven-page list of Black colleges in the *Green Book* was a powerful affront to that reality.

"Negro Schools and Colleges in the United States"

ALABAMA

Birmingham
  Miles Memorial College

Huntsville
  Oakwood College

Selma
  Selma University

Montgomery
  State Teachers College

Tuscaloosa
  Stillman Institute

Talladega
  Talladega College

Tuskegee
  Tuskegee Normal and
    Industrial Institute

ARKANSAS

Pine Bluff
  Agricultural Mechanical, and
    Normal College

Little Rock
  Arkansas Baptist College
  Dunbar Junior College
  Philander Smith College

North Little Rock
  Shorter College

DELAWARE

Dover
  State College for Colored
    Students

DISTRICT OF COLUMBIA

Washington
  Howard University
  Miner Teachers College

FLORIDA

Daytona Beach
  Bethune-Cookman College

Jacksonville
  Edward Waters College

St. Augustine
  Florida Normal and Industrial
    Institute

Tallahassee
  Florida Agricultural and
    Mechanical College

GEORGIA

Atlanta
  Atlanta School of Social Work
  Atlanta University
  Morehouse College
  Spelman College
  Clark University
  Gammon Theological Seminary
  Morris Brown University

Albany
  Georgia Normal and Agricultural
    College

Augusta
  Paine College

Fort Valley
  Fort Valley Normal and
    Industrial School

Industrial College
  Georgia State College

KENTUCKY

Frankfort
  Kentucky State Industrial
    College

Louisville
  Louisville Municipal College for
    Negroes

LOUISIANA

New Orleans
  Dillard University
  Xavier University

Baker
  Leland College

Grambling
  Louisiana Normal and
    Industrial Institute

Scotlandville
  Southern University and Agri-
    cultural and Mechanical College

4

An article reprinted from the *New York Times* entitled "Money for Negro Colleges" preceded the list of schools in the *Green Book*. John D. Rockefeller (the CEO of Esso) was the chairman of the advisory committee at the United Negro College Fund, which he founded in 1944. The article featured his campaign to raise 1.3 million dollars for Black colleges and stated, "The need for full subscription is more pressing this year because of the unusual burden thrown on all educational facilities by the returning veteran. The Negro played an important and often heroic part in the war. He shared the mud, the danger, the sweat, and the tears. Now he has the right to continue his interrupted education if he wants to do so. Many college doors will be closed to him, and to others regardless of race, color, or creed, simply because there are too many returning veterans to be cared for at once in the colleges of their choice. But we cannot allow these thirty-three Negro private colleges to turn away any applicant because they lack funds or to curtail their programs because of it."

The article reminded readers that educating Black citizens would uplift all Americans when it stated, "The educated Negro was once a rarity. His numbers are increasing year by year, and his contributions to the arts, sciences, and education steadily gain a wider and just recognition for his abilities. From these, we all gain, regardless of color. And, as we mutually put a proper, unprejudiced estimate on the contributions of all races to the common good, we move surely closer to the goal of living together in harmony."

In addition to educational services, the GI Bill also offered housing and employment to WWII veterans. From 1944 to 1971, the U.S. government spent nearly one hundred billion dollars on this project. Education provided better jobs and better salaries. Unfortunately, again, most Black WWII veterans didn't benefit from these services. Although there was no language explicitly denying them access, they rarely had the opportunities that were so freely given to whites because the government left the allocation of funds up to the states. For example, only two Black men were recipients of the 3,229 Veterans Administration loans distributed over thirteen Mississippi cities in 1947.

Additionally, the GI Bill gave veterans low-interest home loans, requiring no down payment, but few Black men benefited from this because they needed a bank to approve the loan, and banks were notorious for routinely denying loans to Black men.

There were three banks listed in all the *Green Book*s over the life of the guide: the New Age Federal Savings and Loan Association in St. Louis, Missouri, and two branches of the Carver Federal Savings and Loan Association in New York City, one in Brooklyn and one in Harlem. Although they were listed, these banks didn't advertise in the *Green Book* until 1959,

Carver Federal Savings Bank, a former *Green Book* site in Harlem, New York, 2016

so unfortunately, they were not known to most Black World War II veterans who should have profited from the GI Bill in the late 1940s.

It was the most comprehensive initiative set forth by the government and is often credited with creating the white middle class. Today, many of the homes that white veterans bought with the help of the GI Bill are worth at least ten times their purchase price and have provided financial security, retirement, and college tuition for generations of the same family. Black GIs being denied access to this entitlement program is one of the reasons why today the average white American family has nearly ten times the net worth of the average Black American family.

Although the 1946 and 1947 *Green Book* editions tackled serious topics such as war and education, Green lightened the tone with a series of articles dedicated to classic American cars. Cars were, after all, at the heart of the *Green Book*, and he featured all the popular makes, including Chevrolet, Pontiac, Buick, Oldsmobile, and Cadillac. The section goes on for thirteen pages and is replete with details about armrests, ashtrays, and engines. Green believed the car was the one thing Black people could control regarding their freedom; if they had a car, they wouldn't be subjected to the insults and dangers of segregated travel.

This is Cadillac's 62 Model

Cadillac's 62 Model, *Green Book*, 1947

Irene Morgan

Having a car would have saved Irene Morgan a lot of grief and heartache in 1944, eleven years before Rosa Parks famously refused to give up her seat to a white passenger in Montgomery, Alabama. Morgan, who worked in a factory that built World War II bombers, was traveling on a bus in Gloucester County, Virginia. She wasn't feeling well that day, so when the bus driver instructed her to give up her seat to a white person when they reached Saluda, Virginia, she refused. After the police arrived, Morgan stood her ground. When the officer tried to grab her, she kicked him, clawed at him, and tore his clothes. "He was blue and purple and turned all colors," she remembered. "I started to bite him, but he looked dirty."

Morgan was arrested and thrown in jail. She pled guilty to resisting arrest but not guilty to violating the Virginia segregation law. Future Supreme Court justice Thurgood Marshall argued her case. It was appealed all the way to the Supreme Court, and she won. The *Irene Morgan v. Commonwealth of Virginia* decision made segregation on interstate transportation vehicles illegal, and one year later, sixteen civil rights activists tested the law, riding buses and trains south in the first "Freedom Ride." Regardless of the ruling, there were several arrests, and segregation was still widely practiced. But the Morgan case was critical because it called attention to the atrocities of segregated travel and was a key predecessor to the Freedom Rides.

The Benjamin Franklin, a former *Green Book* hotel in Philadelphia, Pennsylvania

The Morgan case led to symbolic strides in Washington, but travel by bus or train was still a degrading and perilous experience for Black people. Even the baseball legend Jackie Robinson suffered humiliating acts of discrimination after he was chosen as the first African American to play in the Major Leagues since Moses Fleetwood Walker in 1884. Robinson couldn't speak publicly about the unfair treatment he often encountered because he had signed a contract agreeing to look the other way when he was racially victimized, something that happened often when he was traveling.

There is no evidence that Robinson used the *Green Book*, though it would have been useful when he and his teammates from the Brooklyn Dodgers were refused service at the Benjamin Franklin Hotel in Philadelphia, Pennsylvania. The hotel manager told the team's traveling secretary, Harold Parrott, "Don't bring your team back here while you have any Nigras with you!" Ironically, the same Benjamin Franklin Hotel was listed in the *Green Book* about five years later, in the 1952 edition.

Chapter 4

A LICENSE TO LEAVE

I n the first three decades of the twentieth century, at least one lynching of a Black person took place every four days in the South. Most of these horrific, brutal massacres didn't happen deep in the woods, hidden from sight. They were state-sanctioned events that took place in public squares and on courthouse lawns. Earl Hutchinson, a Black man who left the South in the 1940s, recalls in his book *A Colored Man's Journey Through 20th Century Segregated America*, published in 2000, "By the time I was ten-years-old

Green Book cover, 1949

The Negro Motorist
GREEN BOOK

AN INTERNATIONAL TRAVEL GUIDE
U. S. A. ALASKA BERMUDA MEXICO CANADA
1949 EDITION

Carry your Green Book with you - You may need it.

Travel Is Fatal To Prejudice —
MARK TWAIN

Travel Strengthens America —

more than one thousand Blacks had been lynched. Lynch mobs riddled their colored victims with bullets, burned them at the stake, and hacked them to pieces. Often a whole town of whites would turn out to see a lynching . . . Some would pack picnic lunches, and politicians and some businesspersons would show up to make speeches. In some places, they put advertisements in local newspapers announcing the lynching."

An infamous lynching was the murder of Rubin Stacy in Fort Lauderdale, Florida, in 1935, the year the first *Green Book* was being developed. The lynching is memorialized in a photograph featuring Stacy's bullet-ridden body and nine white onlookers: three men, two women, and four young girls in pristine white dresses. One child is smiling as she watches Stacy's body

hanging from the tree. One hundred thousand copies of the photograph were distributed and sold as postcards.

Between 1877 and 1968, the Ku Klux Klan and other white vigilante gangs casually massacred more than four thousand

The lynching of tenant farmer Rubin Stacy in Fort Lauderdale, Florida (July 19, 1935). Printed in a NAACP pamphlet. Postcards were regularly sold at lynchings to commemorate the events.

Black people. Earl Hutchinson read the *Chicago Defender* to stay informed. If there was a lynching, he said, "the *Defender* would provide a detailed account of it." By the time the 1948 *Green Book* was published, nearly two hundred anti-lynching laws had been proposed in Congress. Given that none of them had passed, it was clear the federal government wasn't going to do anything to stop the terrorism.

Considering that the majority of the lynchings were happening in the South, it's no wonder that Black southerners sought refuge in the northern and western reaches of the country—and the *Green Book* was the perfect tool to facilitate this mass migration. It likely also gave Black southerners the courage they needed to leave.

Over the thirty years the *Green Book* was in publication, more than five million Black Americans headed north. Most history books say the Great Migration happened because Black southerners were seeking better job opportunities, and although this was partially true, it's critical to remember that they were primarily fleeing white supremacy and racial terror.

Lynchings didn't scare only Black Americans into leaving. An article written in the *Defender* in 1936 suggested that Charles Lindbergh—a white man celebrated for making the first solo transatlantic flight in 1927—left the United States because he was so disturbed by "the complacent [*sic*] with which America has accepted brutal lynchings of scores of Negroes annually." In that same issue, the *Defender* published a cartoon of the celebrated aviator leaving America on a boat headed to England. In the cartoon, Lindy, waving goodbye, says, "America is too lawless. We lived in constant terror and embarrassment." A well-dressed Black family stands on the shore watching Lindbergh sail

Thomas Rice playing Jim Crow in blackface, New York City, 1833

away, saying, "We can understand how you feel 'Lindy.'" As long as lynchings were happening and Jim Crow was the law of the land, there was no reason to stay in the South.

The term *Jim Crow* didn't start out as a set of laws to racially divide the South; it was initially the name for a stage character played by a white man named Thomas Dartmouth Rice. In the 1830s, Rice was known as "Daddy Rice" and was called the "father of Blackface." Modeling his character after a physically disabled slave, Rice blackened his face and danced in tattered clothes, a disheveled hat, and ragged shoes while singing, "Every time I turn about, I jump Jim Crow." He wasn't the first white man to perform in blackface, but his imitation of a dimwitted, coal-colored slave became a national sensation that influenced the stage well into the 1940s. Rice's legacy fueled harmful stereotypes that made life increasingly unbearable for Black southerners.

The Great Migration was the most massive internal resettlement of any group of people in the United States and, possibly, the world. Starting in 1916 millions of Black southerners gathered up everything they could carry and collected every ounce of courage they had—and left. It lasted from 1916 until 1970, with migrants following three well-traveled routes. Southeastern Black people from Florida, the Carolinas, and Virginia traveled north along the Atlantic coast to Pennsylvania and New England. The second lane of Black southerners left from Kentucky, Tennessee, Alabama, and Mississippi to settle in St. Louis, Chicago, and Detroit. And the third group of migrants left Texas, Louisiana, and Arkansas and headed west to Los Angeles, California.

Black family migrating from the South to Chicago

Approximately 1.5 million Black southerners migrated from 1916 to 1929. Many traveled north during and after World War I because the North was hiring cheap labor. Northern companies had previously hired European immigrants to do factory work, but once the migration from Europe slowed

"No Dogs, Negroes, Mexicans." Printed Jim Crow sign, Lonestar Restaurant Association, Dallas, Texas.

down, the North recruited southern Blacks to fill the labor gap. When the southern counties realized that so many Black residents were leaving the South, they weren't willing to give up their cheap labor without a fight, so they made it difficult for Black southerners to leave. In some cases, those who tried to leave were arrested on train platforms, and when there were too many people to arrest, the train was waved through, prevented from even stopping at the station.

Those who made it onto a train had a difficult journey ahead of them. They were seated in the Jim Crow car, the first car, near the engine, the loudest, dirtiest, and most uncomfortable place to sit. By the end of the ride, the coal dust from the engine covered Black passengers, ruining their clothes. Meanwhile the white passengers, who had paid the same fare, were seated in cars farther back, where they could breathe fresh, clean air in the comfort of heated, reclining chairs with adjustable arm- and footrests.

Not every train was segregated, but even integrated travel was stressful for Black travelers. Earlean Lindsey, who migrated north, said that when there were white people on the train, "the conductor would tell us when you get to Kentucky, pull down the shades because if there were Black and white folks sitting in the same motor coach people would throw bricks at the train window."

Ramona Green, Victor Green's sister-in-law, remembers, "My father worked at a railroad in Chicago, so we usually traveled by train during the summer months. From Chicago to St. Louis, we'd leave on a beautiful train; at St. Louis we'd get off onto these dilapidated cars . . . Everything was so different because we crossed the Mason-Dixon line."

Train travel was not comfortable for Black people, so those who could afford it, drove. And many of them brought the *Green Book* along with them. As Hutchinson wrote, "The *Green Book* was the bible of every Negro highway traveler . . . You literally didn't dare leave home without it."

Although their primary reason for leaving the South was to live a life free from racial terror, Black migrants were also seeking financial stability. During the 1940s the average Black family's annual income was about half that of white families. Although roughly 1 percent of the Black migrants were wealthy—mostly composed of physicians, dentists, lawyers, and entertainers— most were poor.

Still, leaving the South didn't guarantee financial success. In fact, only roughly 10 percent of the Black families in the North were paid the same as whites. In 1941 A. Philip Randolph, a prominent civil rights leader and labor activist, called on Eleanor Roosevelt to pressure her husband, President Roosevelt, to desegregate the defense industry. As a result, Black migrants found stable manufacturing jobs in Chicago, Cleveland, Detroit, Los Angeles, and New York City. The lumber industry was also a solid employment option.

Northern wages weren't automatically higher for all Black workers. Some Black engineers and carpenters had actually made more money in the South, but again, the terror of white supremacy was so relentless that the few Black people who held these skilled jobs opted to trade money for dignity, deciding that they were better off working as a janitor in the North. John George Van

"Colored" sign at a bus station in Rome, Georgia, 1943

Deusen, in his book *The Black Man in White America*, writes, "Despite social and political discrimination, it is a mistake to assume, as many people do, that the Negro is better off in the northern than in the southern states. In the North the colored man may ride in the same streetcar and send his children to the same schools with white people; but he is always subject to economic restriction. He is no longer secure in industry. Generally speaking, he is permitted to work only in menial pursuits and ill-paid callings undesired by the whites. Such discrimination is the most drastic of all discrimination because it determines his income and permanently denies to himself and his family an opportunity to raise their cultural standards."

Like any group of people who leave their homeland, the driving force that propels them forward is the belief that their new life will be better than the one they left behind. And although most Black southerners knew what they were running from, most of them had no idea what they were running to. After crossing the Mason-Dixon line, they quickly learned that Jim Crow had no borders. Yes, there were fewer WHITES ONLY signs, but many of the towns they passed through held the same fearful and ignorant attitudes toward them that were prevalent in the South. Also, they found they couldn't eat, sleep, or get gas in many white-owned businesses, so all the ice coolers, portable toilets, bedding, and gas cans they had used to travel around the South were still needed.

Although the *Green Book* offered peace of mind, it wasn't a cure-all. Several areas of the country weren't represented, and renting a room at a random roadside motel was not easy. Hutchinson remembers, "[If] I spotted a vacancy sign at a motel not listed in the *Green Book* and there were few cars in the motel lot, I would try to get a room. In most cases, the clerk had an arsenal of excuses ready: 'Sorry, forgot to change the sign,' 'The last room was just rented,' 'We're expecting a large group to check in later.'"

The western United States had the least number of *Green Book* accommodations compared to other parts of the country, and Victor Green did everything he could to expand the guide. It was harder to secure listings in the West mostly because there were simply fewer Black business owners there. Until 1940 only about 10 percent of Black migrants made the trip west, but after 1940 that number increased twofold. As more Black people moved west, Green sent letters to hotel and restaurant owners in several western cities asking if they would advertise in his guide.

North Dakota was the only state that had no listings at all in the 1948 *Green Book*. Green reprinted a letter he'd received from a man in Dickinson, North Dakota, attempting to explain why Green was having such a hard time finding businesses to advertise in the guide. The man wrote, "Several places of business, while they are glad to provide for Negro customers, do not care to advertise for Negro trade . . . while they themselves had no color prejudices, some of their regular customers did have." He continued: "Ignorance is the root of prejudice . . . There are so few Negroes living in North Dakota that a colored person is still a curiosity. Some of the prejudice here is merely unfamiliarity with any of the race . . . When talking about Negroes, abstractly, they feel differently than if a colored person, in person, asks them for services."

Because the *Green Book* wasn't as useful out west, Black travelers had to build up a tough skin and stockpile a broad range of well-honed survival skills and techniques to handle any hostile situation they might encounter. One strategy was to learn as much as they could about the places they were driving through, by word of mouth or from reading the *Chicago Defender*.

Langston Hughes wrote in the *Chicago Defender* in 1946, "Since I travel about the country a great deal, people are always asking me if I notice any improvement in race relations, if things are better or worse. To tell the truth, I really do not know if they have improved or not. Race relations look like a see-saw to me—up on one end and down on the other, up here and down there, up and down. If one community reports better race relations than before the war, another reports worse." It was a time when the pendulum of progress was swinging both ways.

No matter where Black migrants traveled, service wasn't guaranteed. This was true even at Esso fueling stations. A WE DO NOT CATER TO COLORED sign was posted at one Esso station, near Joliet, Illinois. Although Esso generally supported Black customers, since the stations were privately owned, it was difficult to enforce its values of racial equality. When this racist sign came to the attention of Conger Reynolds, Esso's director of public relations, he had it removed. But just because the sign was changed, the people who put it there hadn't.

"We Want White Tenants," Detroit, Michigan, 1942

Joliet was a rural Illinois town on Route 66, and though Black migrants hoped northern urban areas would be less racist, bigotry and intolerance were rampant there as well. Hutchinson noticed this farther north when he said, "St. Louis suddenly began to look smaller and more provincial than ever to me. It was pretty much a deep southern town. Colored people still couldn't work in stores or offices downtown, and could not eat in restaurants or go to clubs. They could not use any of the libraries, swimming pools, or recreation facilities. Many Negroes still lived in overcrowded, wretched flats, with no running water or inside toilets."

Although many Black migrants who traveled north had to live in slums, the knowledge that they were escaping the Ku Klux Klan kept millions more on the road. Unfortunately, what they didn't realize was that Klan membership had spread like typhoid in the 1920s, throughout the entire country. Reports during this time found that one-quarter of all white males in the state of Indiana were Klansmen.

The Ku Klux Klan had a stronghold in Detroit, one of the top ten cities Black migrants traveled to during the Great Migration, from 1940 until 1970. Black southerners were attracted to the Motor City's plethora of manufacturing and automobile jobs. Although many found employment, most had trouble getting housing. Detroit had undergone a major shift since the 1920s, when the city was 96 percent white. As the auto industry grew, producing solid, well-paying jobs, Black people moved there in droves; by 1943, the Black population had quadrupled. But they weren't alone in taking advantage of the job opportunities: Poor white southerners also moved there—and brought their racist attitudes with them. Southern whites and bigoted locals alike refused to work alongside or live next to Black people, which made it very difficult for Black newcomers to find housing. As a result, Black people were confined to living in a sixty-block stretch on the east side of town.

Mobs of white vigilantes harassed those who tried to settle outside this area; fights broke out, and crosses were burned in Black residents' yards. In 1941 the city built a wall (six feet high, a foot thick, and a half-mile long) to keep Blacks out of a neighborhood that had been zoned as an all-white subdivision—essentially making it a sundown suburb. Detroit's racial tensions boiled under the surface for years, until 1943, when one of the worst race riots of the World War II era erupted. Six thousand army troops were called in to stop the violence, seven hundred people were injured, and thirty-four people died.

Children standing in front of a segregation wall in Detroit, Michigan, 1941

West of Detroit, Chicago was another one of the top ten cities where Black southerners settled during the Great Migration. From the 1940s to the 1960s, its Black population nearly tripled, from approximately 275,000 to more than 800,000. Also, as in Detroit, housing was an explosive issue that caused division and violence. The Chicago suburb of Cicero was notorious for its hostility toward Black people, so it wasn't surprising when, in 1951, a riot broke out there. After a Black family rented an apartment in the neighborhood, a mob of roughly four thousand white people firebombed the building. The rioters were never charged. Even worse, the rental agent and the family's attorney were charged with conspiracy to lower property values.

Housing was and continues to be the most shocking form of overt racial disparity in the nation. The Fair Housing Act protects people from

Bronzeville, Chicago, featured in the *Green Book*, 1949

discrimination when they seek to rent or buy a home, obtain a mortgage, and have other housing issues. It was not passed until after the Civil Rights Act of 1964—which ended segregation in public places and banned employment discrimination—and the Voting Rights Act of 1965, which prohibits racial discrimination in voting. Even white people who didn't consider themselves racist didn't want Black neighbors. The Fair Housing Act finally passed in April 1968. It was the last of the critical pieces of civil rights legislation to be passed in the 1960s, seven days after Martin Luther King Jr. was assassinated.

Black migrants who moved to Chicago were practically forced to live on either the West or the South Side of the city. Thankfully, the *Green Book* listed more than 180 businesses in Chicago, with nearly 80 percent of the listings in the Bronzeville District. This was a vibrant area in the South Side. Three hundred fifty thousand Black people lived, ate, shopped, and worked here. It was also a mecca for Black manufacturing, and the Black hair care, publishing, and banking industries. The 1949 *Green Book* featured a seven-page article spotlighting Bronzeville, with a full-page image

REGAL

of the South Center department store, which employed two hundred Black workers; the Mutual Assurance Company; the Metropolitan Funeral Parlor; and the Supreme Liberty Life Insurance building (at the time, Liberty Life was the third-largest Black insurance company in America). Victor Green proudly called these places "monuments to Negro business."

As long as there were no COLORED or WHITES ONLY signs, the northern states believed they were better than the Jim Crow South. But racialized space was alive and well in Chicago. Once Earl Hutchinson arrived there, he said, "It didn't take long for me to discover that Chicago was no promised land either. Regardless of their income or status, Negroes could only live on the Southside [*sic*] north of 43rd to 29th streets between Ellis Avenue on the east, and Wentworth Avenue on the west and in another area called the Westside . . . If a cop stopped you for anything, you had to shove a dollar in his hand. It was a racket, and everyone knew it, and went along with it."

Earlean Lindsey, another Chicago migrant, started to learn some of the rules: "We could not go across Cottage Grove. It was off-limits. I worked at the University of Chicago . . . and we used to have to wear badges. People think this is a lie, but this is the truth: [We had] to show why we were in that area at a certain time of night."

Curtis Coleman, who migrated to Chicago in 1944, summed up his experience by saying, "Well, in the South you knew the law, they told you the truth. Chicago, they won't tell you the truth. That's the only difference."

It didn't take long for Black southerners to realize that they were settling into an area governed by policies that had kept Black Americans anchored in a northern caste system not too different from the one they left in the South.

And this wasn't unique to Chicago. Every major American city that attracted Black southerners had (and still has) hypersegregated neighborhoods, due primarily to heavy policing, predatory lending practices (such as making Blacks pay exorbitant interest rates), and real estate redlining.

The Federal Housing Administration (FHA) is a U.S. government agency within the U.S. Department of Housing and Urban Development (HUD) that provides mortgage insurance on home loans that are made by FHA-approved lenders such as banks and mortgage companies. It graded communities based on their racial demographics and essentially "redlined" them, meaning the areas where Black people lived were marked red and labeled "D," a lower grade, indicating a "high-risk" community. A typical statement in the mortgage read, "At no time shall said premises . . . be sold, occupied, let or leased . . . to anyone of any race other than the Caucasian, except that this covenant shall not prevent occupancy by domestic servants of a different race domiciled with an owner or tenant." Black migrants learned that most of the northern and western states didn't need WHITES ONLY signs because the government's housing policies—where Black people could live and if and how they could rent or buy a home—separated the races for them.

For Black migrants who couldn't find adequate housing up north or who wanted to avoid living in a Chicago ghetto, the 1949 edition of the *Green Book* was a welcome sight, publishing an article on Robbins, a semirural all-Black town south of Chicago that was owned and operated by Black people.

From Reconstruction up to World War I, there were at least sixty Black towns in the United States. During the time the Green Book was published, Black towns weren't as plentiful, but Robbins, Illinois, was booming.

The population rose from just under five hundred people in the 1920s to approximately thirteen thousand in the 1940s. And 90 percent of its residents were homeowners.

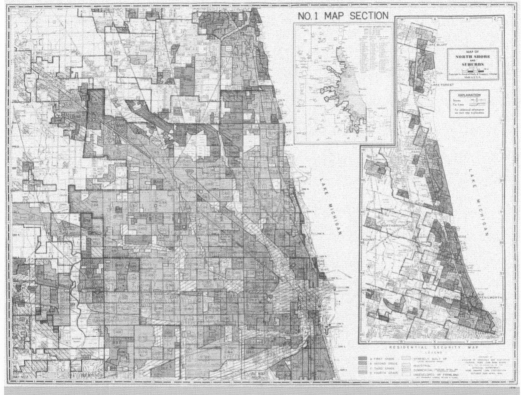

Chicago redlining map, 1940. The areas in red designate Black neighborhoods.

Robbins was a source of pride in the Black community. The town opened the first U.S. airport to be owned and operated by Blacks and housed the nation's only flight school for Black people, which ultimately inspired the Tuskegee Airmen program—a group of Black military pilots and airmen who fought in World War II.

Unfortunately, by the 1970s, due to massive layoffs at nearby factories, Robbins slid into decline, and it was nearly bankrupt by the late 1980s. What happened in Robbins was happening across the North. Industries that had attracted Black migrants started moving to the suburbs and then overseas, to outsource their labor. By the mid-1980s, more than half a million Black people left the North and returned to the South, where housing, taxes, and education were more affordable.

Still, before it met its end, Robbins was celebrated in the *Green Book* as a place without prejudice and a viable alternative for Black people who wanted to live in a vibrant, self-sustaining community. It was a glowing example of resiliency and empowerment, and a beacon of light for those traveling on the road to freedom. This is what Black people were looking for when they left the South. They were seeking political asylum and protection under the law, and the *Green Book* became their passport. It was a license to leave.

The Negro Motorist Green Book

An International Travel Guide

Carry Your Green Book With You You May Need It.	1950 Edition	Price $1.00

Chapter 5

ALL ABOARD

On the cover of the 1950 *Green Book*, a fair-skinned, well-dressed Black woman in a stylish feathered hat stands in New York City's Penn Station looking at train schedules. She appears to be heading west, because she's holding a pamphlet for a Pacific-bound train. Each mile west still symbolized an opportunity for a better life. In the mythology that gave us the American Dream, the West has always represented freedom. And once you reached the westernmost edge of the continent, there was

Green Book cover, 1950

California—there you could relax in the land of swaying palm trees framed by a cerulean blue ocean, while ripe fruit fell to the ground under a sunlit sky. It was the place where dreams could come true.

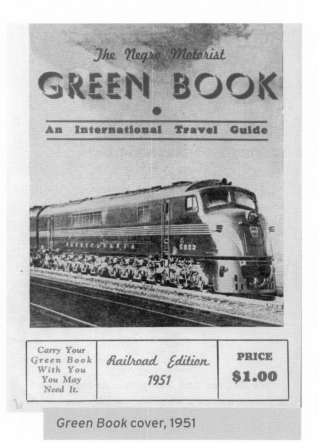

Green Book cover, 1951

It was easy to idolize the West because it was a faraway land where most Black people didn't live. In the late 1940s, this began to change. More and more Black people, especially those who lived in Texas and Arkansas, headed to California. By the 1950s, just like the West, the train became a symbol of progress for Black Americans. If you could afford a ticket, you could change your life.

The train was also an intimate part of the Black community, as the Pullman Company had long been the largest private employer of African Americans in the country. Those who didn't work for the railroad likely knew someone who did. Black men worked on trains as dining car chefs, busboys, and mechanics, but most of them were porters. The job entailed assisting passengers at stations and while on board. Being a Pullman porter was considered an honorable job, one that symbolized success, as it provided a stable middle-class lifestyle.

The train was such an important part of the Black community that Victor Green dedicated the entire 1951 edition to it, naming it the "Railroad Edition." He opens the 1951 issue with a six-page, fully illustrated article, "The American Railroad," featuring photographs of Black porters standing at attention in a dining car and assisting white passengers sitting in plush velvet seats. Traveling throughout the country dressed in starched white shirts and black bowties had elevated the porter's status from servant to ambassador. By the 1950s, the porter had become an icon of American travel.

As porters traveled throughout the country, they spread the word about the latest news in Black culture, passing out the *Chicago Defender* and the latest copies of the *Green Book*. They were also well versed in the latest trends in music, food, and politics from coast to coast.

When porters weren't on trains, a popular place for them to socialize was at the headquarters for the Brotherhood of Sleeping Car Porters union in Boston. Images of trains lined the walls, and there were a few cots, some lockers, a desk, a typewriter, and a pool table.

The Brotherhood of Sleeping Car Porters was founded by A. Philip Randolph, the same civil rights and labor activist who had helped persuade President Roosevelt to desegregate the defense industry. Randolph fought hard for all Black train workers, men and women. This was especially critical because, although employment as a porter was considered a good job, most porters were exploited for their labor. The average porter functioned on four hours of sleep, working four hundred hours a month in twenty-hour stints. The Black maids who worked on trains weren't treated any better. Train maids helped white female passengers bathe, gave them manicures, did their

Individual reading lights may be beamed directly to each seat in Northern Pacific's new streamlined coaches now in service on the North Coast Limited.

about 3,700 new passenger-train cars have been installed, and these are improved in almost every way over those in use even a decade ago.

These cars, along with the other modern cars in service and those being continually installed, go a long way in making rail travel more comfortable and convenient than ever before. Whether the trip be in a coach or a sleeping car, every effort has been made to assure a more pleasant journey.

Fluorescent lighting bathes the interior of these new cars with glareless, even light, and many cars feature individually controlled lights. Careful attention has been given to interior decoration of cars, and they have restful color combinations such as blue, grey and ivory walls and

ceilings and with rose upholstery and carpets.

Seating facilities in the new coaches offer all the comfort that improved design can give them. Reclining seats with adjustable footrests invite relaxation, and many seats can be swung around to provide a clear, unobstructed view of the countryside through wide windows.

Coach lounges are larger and more luxurious, and have comfortable chairs, large mirrors and additional wash basins. Electro-pneumatic devices cause doors to open at the touch of a finger and remain open until the traveler has passed.

Public address systems carry announcements, music and radio programs of interest through many trains.

Spaciousness is the keynote of new coaches. This greater space for each passenger is reflected in such things as more leg room between seats and

CLUB DINER "LA FIESTA" on Rock Island's streamliner The Golden State.

hair, and looked after their children. Some even acted as nursemaids if a passenger became ill. Essentially, both the porters and maids were at white passengers' beck and call.

Randolph's was the first Black union to sign a collective bargaining agreement with a major corporation. It guaranteed the rights of both the male and female employees. He secured the most substantial wage increase the porters had ever received and made sure they were offered fair compensation for the hours between their shifts while they were still on the trains. As a result of his efforts, the porters' workload was reduced from four hundred hours a month to two hundred forty.

The Brotherhood of Sleeping Car Porters was located right upstairs from Charlie's Sandwich Shoppe, a restaurant listed in the *Green Book* for fifteen years and still open today. Charlie Poulous and his hardworking Greek immigrant family started the restaurant in 1927. Charlie's was an unusual *Green Book* site because it was white-owned and served Black folks in Boston's mostly white South End. Some white locals refused to eat at the restaurant because they didn't want to sit next to Black people. By integrating the space, Charlie set the tone, one of respect and tolerance. And if he lost business because he served Black folks, he didn't care. His humanity wasn't for sale.

Denver was featured in the 1950 edition of the *Green Book*. Although the article lists tourist sites located downtown, most of the hotels downtown wouldn't serve Black people. So 90 percent of Denver's eighty-seven *Green Book* listings for that year are clustered in the Five Points neighborhood.

Denver's Five Points district played an important role for Black travelers heading west. In most western cities, Black people comprised only about

3 percent of the population. This wasn't true for Five Points. In 1870 there were roughly two hundred Black residents, but by 1920, there were more than five thousand, making it one of the largest African American communities west of the Mississippi River. And because there were so few options for Black people to stay in that area of the country, Five Points was a necessary stopping place for Black migrants traveling west.

Five Points had more Black-owned businesses than any neighborhood outside Harlem, which is why it was called the "Harlem of the West." Other neighborhoods in western cities were called the "Harlem of the West," but Five Points deserved the title. It featured three Black-owned newspapers and scores of other Black-owned businesses, including barbershops, grocery stores, tailors, movie theaters, restaurants, drugstores, jazz clubs, dressmakers, hotels, and real estate offices. Black doctors, lawyers, and musicians called Five Points home, but one of its most famous residents was probably businesswoman, philanthropist, and activist Madam C. J. Walker, who moved there in 1905 and became a millionaire with her Black hair care products. The neighborhood was so popular that, in some circles, it was considered its own city. Letters addressed to "Five Points, Colorado" (instead of "Denver") were delivered with no problem.

The Rossonian, a *Green Book* hotel listed from 1939 to 1955, hosted a variety of celebrities, such as Billie Holiday, Ella Fitzgerald, and Charlie Parker. Out of all the *Green Book* sites listed in Five Points, the Rossonian is the only one still operating today.

A landmark hotel and jazz club, the Rossonian sat at the center of the five converging streets after which the neighborhood is named. The

Beaux-Arts–style 13,500-square-foot building is visually stunning. Like the famous Flatiron Building in New York City, it is wedge-shaped, wide in the back and then narrowed down to almost a point at the front door. It opened as the Baxter Hotel in 1912 and was renamed the Rossonian in 1929. It was considered one of the best jazz clubs between Kansas City and Los Angeles; musicians loved it. After playing downtown to white audiences, they'd head to the Rossonian, which became a regular stop for after-hours jam sessions.

In the late 1950s, when some of the racially restrictive housing covenants were lifted in Denver, the city became less segregated. But as African Americans with money left Five Points to live in more affluent

The Rossonian, a former *Green Book* hotel and nightclub in Denver, Colorado, 2018

neighborhoods in the city, and Black celebrity tourists could now stay in downtown hotels, the neighborhood fell into decline.

The Five Points neighborhood was designated the "Five Points Historic Cultural District" in 2015. Even though Five Points had been the heart of the city's African American community—a plaque commemorating this history is displayed across the street from the Rossonian—most of the neighborhood's original residents have been pushed out, to be replaced by white urbanites. Nearly all of Five Points' Black-owned *Green Book* businesses are now white-owned microbreweries, bakeries, coffee shops, or dog parks.

Though not much is left of its historic past, in its prime the city of Denver was a mecca for Black travelers. It was the first major city that Black migrants encountered in the West. Traveling farther west, however, wasn't easy. As the landscape became more desolate, and people found themselves driving on long, deserted roads, food and lodging options became scarce, even for white motorists. So, one of the safest ways to travel west (outside of flying) was to get there by train. Unlike the automobile, railroad cars wouldn't overheat in the middle of the Mojave Desert. And once passengers reached the Southwest, they could find quality food at one of the Harvey House lunchrooms conveniently located in train stations.

Fred Harvey was an ambitious entrepreneur from England. From the late 1800s to the 1960s, rail passengers could find his Harvey Houses in stations along the Atchison, Topeka, and Santa Fe railway lines. When the trains pulled into the station, passengers could step inside a Harvey House and be served a gourmet meal at reasonable prices. Harvey Houses weren't listed in the *Green Book*, but they were known for treating Black travelers with dignity. Not only did Black customers not have to use a back entrance or look for a "Colored" section, but they also received a warm welcome. Compared to eating the roadside slop dished out of trailers in most small western towns at the time, dining at a Harvey House was like attending a royal feast—and best of all, Black customers could eat oysters on the half shell right alongside everyone else.

Whether Black train passengers were escaping Jim Crow or merely taking a vacation, Los Angeles was often their destination if they were heading west. This is probably why, just five pages after the railroad article in the 1951 edition, Green published a four-page article on Los Angeles.

Casa del Desierto Harvey House in Barstow, California

The article, "The Wonder City: Los Angeles, Calif.," features sweeping images of the highway hugging the Pacific Ocean. It begins with a glowing statement about dreaming of a place with the "perfect climate" offering "beauty" and "wonder." Unfortunately, most Black migrants looking for the American Dream in Los Angeles found the City of Angels even more

The Wonder City
Los Angeles, Calif.

Sometime in everyone's life, there are dreams of traveling either to distant lands, or to see their own land. Some dream of travel by air, some by boat, railway or motor.

Today beautiful highways with conveniently situated stations, bus lines, air-lines and fast trains, make it possible to realize these dreams.

There is much to be seen and more to learn, of this our land which offers everything of beauty, wonder and history.

The city of interminable dimensions, covering some 452 square miles, sometimes alluded to as the "Coney Island of the Pacific," possibly because of its demise attractions, the most outstanding being, its almost perfect climate. It is said that under more than 300 days of sunshine here every year; anything will flourish and develop.

Emigrants to Los Angeles from every Mid-Western State has made it the largest western city of the United States, in fact it is to the west what

ROOSEVELT HIGHWAY skirts the Pacific Ocean and passes through the beach cities in Los Angeles county. this view taken from the palisades a few miles north of Santa Monica, shows one of the many fine stretches of beach which parallel the highway.

Opening page of the Los Angeles article featured in the *Green Book*, 1951

segregated than the South. Peola Denham, who moved there from Baton Rouge, Louisiana, found the neighborhood of Watts, in South Los Angeles, far more segregated than her hometown. Since white merchants ran most of the places Denham had shopped at in Louisiana, she said she saw more white people in Baton Rouge than she did in Los Angeles, where she could live her entire life without ever seeing a white person. With segregation in place in Los Angeles, Black people owned nearly all the stores in Denham's neighborhood. It was clear the city didn't need the formal segregation laws that existed in the Jim Crow South. Los Angeles's strict housing covenants were enough to keep the races divided.

When Earl Hutchinson moved to Los Angeles, he got his real estate license and started working for a Black real estate broker. This gave him a "firsthand look at the rampant racism in housing in Los Angeles. The black real estate brokers were refused membership in the Board of Realtors, which was a trade organization that was aligned with the real estate industry. They didn't give black [r]ealtors an official reason for denying membership." The "single biggest problem that confronted us," he said, "was the practice of redlining." Back then, Hutchinson wrote, "all the major banks such as the Bank of America, Chase Manhattan, American Savings, Union Bank, and many others across the U.S. engaged in the practice."

To help Black migrants, the *Green Book* listed a handful of real estate agents. Hutchinson wasn't listed, but from 1949 to 1955, Bernard C. Herndon's office was. It was located in the heart of South Central.

Like the Five Points district in Denver, Los Angeles's South Central neighborhood was where the majority of Black people lived and played.

South Central hosted more than 80 percent of Los Angeles's 220 *Green Book* accommodations, which were clustered within a three-mile radius. It didn't matter that South Central bordered Culver City, a sundown town. If Black travelers could find their way to South Central, they didn't need to go anywhere else.

South Central in the 1950s was teeming with musicians, writers, politicians, and comics, planting the seeds for a new Black identity in the United States. This vibrant Black enclave influenced a cultural movement that permeated Black fashion, music, and language and laid the groundwork for hip-hop culture. The street scene in South Central and the significant contributions being made to the community during these years birthed a mid-century Harlem Renaissance of the West.

Wealthy and middle-class Black people who visited Los Angeles stayed at the Dunbar Hotel, in South Central, which was listed in the *Green Book* from 1939 to 1961. The adjoining beauty parlor and liquor store were also listed.

The Dunbar was built as the Somerville Hotel in 1928, by a Black dentist named John Alexander, who, after being repeatedly denied service in white hotels, had decided to open his own. It was the first American hotel built expressly for Black people; it featured one hundred rooms and sixty private baths. In 1930, ownership of the hotel passed on to Lucius Lomax and he renamed it the Dunbar, after the African American poet Paul Laurence Dunbar. (Eighteen other *Green Book* sites were also named after the poet.) It wasn't long before it became the cultural and social hub for the Black intelligentsia. W. E. B. Du Bois, Billie Holiday, and Duke Ellington were regulars there. The hotel became the unofficial country club for the Black elite.

Tom Bradley, Los Angeles's first Black mayor, said, "I remember from the days of my childhood, walking down the avenue just to get a look at some of those famous superstars who stayed at The Dunbar." Chicago businessman Jimmy Nelson bought the Dunbar in 1936. Former president of the LA branch of the NAACP and state chairman of the Congress of Racial Equality (CORE), Nelson said, "[C]ivil rights issues were discussed openly every night at the Dunbar."

Dunbar Hotel lobby, a former *Green Book* hotel in Los Angeles, California, 2016

The Dunbar closed in 1974 because it didn't meet the fire codes, and by 1987 it had deteriorated into a graffiti-scarred ruin. It fell into decline during the civil rights movement partially due to integration and likely due

The Regal, a former *Green Book* hotel in Los Angeles, California, 2016

to the fallout from the 1965 Watts riots. In the 1980s, the Community Development Department and the Community Redevelopment Agency of the city of Los Angeles spent 2.9 million dollars renovating the hotel. Today the Dunbar provides seventy-two units of low-income housing for seniors and is safe from demolition because it is listed on the National Register of Historic Places.

Although South Central was the primary hub for *Green Book* businesses in Los Angeles, there were also *Green Book* sites located downtown and in Hollywood. For instance, the Mark Twain Hotel was well known as a cheap Hollywood hotel for struggling artists. When Joe Barbera, the animator for Hanna-Barbera (the animation studio that created the likes of Tom and Jerry, the Flintstones, and Yogi Bear), stayed at the Mark Twain in 1937, he described it as an "enlightened penitentiary." Throughout the time it was listed in the *Green Book*, it maintained its reputation as a low-rent hotel for struggling actors, but during the 1940s and '50s, it also offered relatively safe boarding for Black people, who had few options in the area.

Among all the major cities with fifty or more *Green Book* sites, New York City and Los Angeles have the largest number still in operation. About 10 percent of the Los Angeles sites were located downtown, the most prominent ones being Clifton's Cafeteria and the Regal and Norbo hotels.

When the Regal Hotel opened in 1939, it was called "the Finest Negro Hotel on the Coast." A fabulous gala announced the opening of this "ultra-modern" hotel decorated in "restful" colors and catering to the "highest type of Negro clientele." The Black community rallied around the Regal, and local businesses set up shop inside. In suite 101 Zerita Dress Salon showed an exclusive line of women's suits, gowns, coats, and sportswear. And when the NAACP came to town, the Regal took out an ad in the *Los Angeles Sentinel* to welcome the organization.

Right down the street from the Regal, on the weekends, the Norbo cocktail lounge was jumping twenty-four hours a day. In 1954 the Norbo launched "Jam at Dawn," which started at six a.m., and the cocktail lounge hosted nightly jam sessions with recording artists and Cee Pee Johnson, a sensational bongo player. In the 1970s Norbo Hotel fell into decline, eventually becoming a low-income rooming house.

Victor Green lived in the North, so it's very possible he never experienced travel on Jim Crow trains, since the trains north of the Mason-Dixon line provided the same seating to all passengers regardless of race. The hardships of segregated travel are not displayed in his railroad article, which presents a glorious account of train travel, telling readers that railway cars were "more comfortable and convenient than ever before" with "reclining seats with adjustable foot rests, controlled lights . . . restful color combinations such

Part of the *Green Book* back cover, 1957

as . . . rose upholstery and carpets" and that "every effort has been made to assure a more pleasant journey." In fact, knowing what we know about the realities of Black train travel, today's readers might find his article a tone-deaf, insensitive depiction.

After reading horrific migration stories, it's hard to understand Green's intention in publishing the *Green Book* train article. Since the article was produced in partnership with the Association of American Railroads, it's likely that it was initially written for a white audience and that Green, who wouldn't have had the resources to develop an article on Black train travel all on his own, had simply reprinted this one for his readers.

It's possible that reading stories about the subhuman conditions many Black people endured on trains makes it easy to paint Black train travel with a broad brush and assume it was the same for all Black people. But just like now, middle- and upper-class Black people had a completely different experience living in America than those struggling with poverty. And the experiences of those who lived in the South, North, East, and West were different as well.

There is so little information about who Victor Green was that it's impossible to know what his motives were. Up to this point, none of the previous *Green Book* editions addressed racial discrimination directly, with the exception of the 1947 edition, featuring Rockefeller's letter of support for returning Black soldiers. It is important to remember that leisure travel was an aspirational act for people of any race, but especially for the African American consumer market Green was trying to reach. For the most part, anyone able to take a train was someone who could afford the time and expense to travel. Encouraging Black people to leave everything that was familiar and venture into white American spaces was a radical idea. And although the language of the *Green Book* was sometimes tempered or even silent when it came to matters of race, it's possible that Green's mild, nonthreatening approach was intended. For the most part, the *Green Book* was tailored not to offend, incite, or inflame racial tensions. Victor Green ignored race when he could because his guide was a powerful tool that offered one solution to a problem that everyone already knew existed.

Chapter 6

VACATION

I n 1952 the *Green Book* changed its name from the *Negro Motorist Green Book* to the *Negro Travelers' Green Book*. Victor Green said he changed the name because it was "confusing and a good many people thought it was intended for the motorist only, but is used for any mode of travel." Changing the name signaled that Green was expanding the concept of travel and vacation for Black Americans.

Postcard depicting a street scene at Atlantic Beach, South Carolina

Street Scene at Atlantic Beach, S.C.

RESERVATION BUREAU

Going to take a trip, attend some convention — make sure of your accommodations before you leave.

HOUSING CONDITIONS MAKE THIS NECESSARY

Reservations for all Hotels, Tourist Homes and Vacation Resorts throughout the United States, Alaska, Mexico and Bermuda can be made for you through our Reservation Bureau.

We have contacts with all Hotels, Tourist Homes and Vacation Resorts. Send us a list of the cities that you expect to pass through, the dates wanted, how many in your party and have us make your reservations. Fees are moderate.

Saves You Time and Money — Write Reservation Bureau

VICTOR H. GREEN & CO.
LEONIA, N. J.

Yes! We Can Arrange Your Vacation . . . . .
Everywhere In The United States

CRUISES — TOURS — TICKETS

WEST INDIES CALIFORNIA MEXICO
BERMUDA EUROPE CANADA
AFRICA SOUTH AMERICA

NO SERVICE CHARGE

VICTOR H. GREEN & CO.
LEONIA, N. J.

Victor Green's Reservation Bureau advertisement, 1949

In 1949 Green launched his "Reservation Bureau," teaming up with Maher Travel Bureau in New York City to book trips to the West Indies, Bermuda, Europe, South America, and Africa. The new enterprise was advertised in every *Green Book* from 1949 to 1957, and there was an entire *Green Book* vacation guide published in addition to the annual 1949 edition. It's unknown how much Green's readers used this service, but it offered to help customers obtain passports and visas along with booking their airline, railroad, and steamship journeys. In 1953 the *Green Book* facilitated international travel with its "Airline Edition." Travel for users of the *Green Book* no longer meant only taking a drive to the nearest city or a train across the country; it now also meant expanding one's horizons and crossing an ocean.

Green Book cover, 1953

Green presented flying as the "miracle of modern travel," and it was the perfect mode of travel for those who could afford it. The seven-page article "Air Transportation" that opens the 1953 edition shows planes sitting on the tarmac at New York's LaGuardia Airport and people boarding and deplaning from aircraft right on the runway, as was done in the 1950s.

This was the "golden age" of travel. American Airlines carried approximately nine million passengers to seventy-two cities every day. And because airline fares were becoming more affordable, cross-continental and international travel was within reach for middle-income Americans. Flying was a luxury that people looked forward to. Unlike today, they didn't have to wait in security lines, juggle bags, remove their shoes, get radiated by machines, and squeeze into a tin can with no leg or elbow room. In those days passengers actually *wanted* to get on an airplane. They dressed in their best clothes, and they only needed to show up thirty minutes before their flight. And they enjoyed gourmet in-flight meals on real dinnerware served by flight attendants wearing tailored suits, white gloves, and pillbox hats.

Victor Green had envisioned broadening the scope of the guide when he told readers in the 1948 *Green Book* to "Watch for the addition of Bermuda to our listings for the 1949 edition." And he delivered on his promise. The two-page article describes Bermuda as a gentle place "of coveted ease, unhurried charm, and relaxed living." Traveling to Bermuda was easy, as it was only a three-hour flight from New York, and no passports or visas were required for vacation travel there. The *Green Book* suggested that its readers pack cotton dresses, lightweight suits, Bermuda shorts, white dinner jackets, and tweed or flannel suits. Bermuda was one of the most regularly promoted countries in the *Green Book* and made an appearance in nearly every subsequent edition.

In the 1950s, international travel was becoming more popular in the Black community. *Ebony* magazine referred to Black jet-setters as "dignified American Negroes." They were featured in Black newspapers throughout

BERMUDA

Out in the Mid-Atlantic, south east of the Virginia Capes, beyond the Gulf Stream's flying fish and phosphorus, lie the most famous coral islands in the World. it is the Bermudas . . . less than 20 square miles in size and so formed that in few spots is it possible to get more than a mile away from the sea. The north and south shores are utterly different and might belong to countries hundreds of leagues apart.

The Bermudas, with startling clarity of sunlight, their gentle tropical sea, their special flash of white-washed roofs, pink-tinted walls and flaming poinciana trees, and their island nights glittering with more stars than any other sky in the Atlantic. They are collectively called "Bermuda." Here we find a place of coveted ease, unhurried charm and relaxed living.

Here it may mean building castles in the cleanest pink and white sand on earth, wandering over coral beaches into ocean that is the greenest green, the bluest blue. It may mean cycling along South Shore Road between tall hedges of Oleander, with youngster and picnic lunches safely tucked in a basket on handle bars.

Or it may be the velvety greens and fairways of one of Bermuda's many golf courses. Or where attractive shops show choicest merchandise of the British Empire.

There are many beautifully kept tennis courts, hidden picnic beaches, delightful roads and coral rocks from which a native fisherman's net may be cast, ensnaring everything including prancing sea-horses and mermaids singing! For, like a jewel set in Mid-Atlantic, Bermuda is the wish at sunset and romance is starlight.

HOW DO I GET TO BERMUDA?

You go from one Parish to another by boat, by bicycle, by the small motor car. Everywhere the place is leisurely. The motor car, convenient for visits from one end of the islands to the other, travels (by law) only a few miles faster than average horse and carriage.

You fly by the latest aircraft or

St. Peter's Church, St. Georges

the country, and an article published in *Ebony* showed Black beauticians taking a trip to Europe in 1954 and praised everything from their "mink capes to their good conduct, both of which apparently surprised some Europeans."

One year before the *Ebony* article, Langston Hughes wrote about how differently Black entertainers were treated overseas. "A major difference between the treatment accorded Negro entertainers at home and abroad is that American audiences will loudly applaud performers who they like inside the theater, outside the theater the Negro artist cannot buy a cup of coffee or find a place to sleep . . . Abroad, colored performers live normally as human beings . . ." Jazz age entertainer Josephine Baker, for example, was socially snubbed in America but beloved in Europe.

Perhaps Black entertainers were treated better overseas, but there was no guarantee that they would be treated fairly on their journey there. On July 19, 1954, Ella Fitzgerald, the Queen of Jazz, along with her manager, pianist, and secretary, left San Francisco on a first-class Pan American flight headed to Australia. When they arrived in Honolulu for a temporary stopover, they were refused boarding for the second leg of the trip because they were Black. The flight attendant wouldn't even allow them back on the plane to retrieve their belongings from first class. They were stranded in Honolulu for two days before they could find another flight to Australia. They were so humiliated and embarrassed that Fitzgerald sued Pan Am for violating the Civil Aeronautics Act of 1938. When the case was dismissed, she appealed and won an out-of-court settlement.

Despite the challenges, articles like the ones in *Ebony* and by Langston

Hughes likely inspired Black Americans to consider international travel. But for regular people in the Black community, especially in the South, the logistics of traveling abroad were daunting. After all, if they were flying out of a southern airport, they still faced segregated restrooms, waiting areas, and restaurants. Charles C. Diggs Jr., the first elected Black member of the House of Representatives from Michigan, wrote this letter in 1953 to the president of Continental Airlines, asking him to desegregate U.S. airports:

Dear Mr. Six:

Sometime ago, during the earlier stages of air transportation, I was heartened to find through personal experience that this newer mode of conveyance was not falling into the older pattern of segregation and discrimination established by railroads and bus lines. A recent trip to the South, however, revealed widespread undemocratic practices. Waiting rooms marked "for white only," separate toilet facilities and water fountains, refusal of limousines and taxies to carry Negroes into the nearest community (and I assume from the nearest community to the airport), and discrimination and/or segregation against Negroes in certain airport restaurants—all of these incidents I witnessed with my own eyes.

At the airport servicing Chattanoga [sic], I experienced the strange paradox of permitting Negroes to eat in the restaurant without restrictions, but prohibiting them from using the same toilet facilities as white people. It appears that we can consume food and beverages in the same place, but we must eliminate same in separate facilities. I understand this is also true at the airport servicing Jacksonville, Florida.

In view of the foregoing circumstances, consider this a formal complaint against these practices and a strong, urgent request that through the influence of your agency and the airlines their cessation be immediately demanded.

Trusting you will handle this matter with dispatch and vigor, I remain

> Very truly yours,
> Charles C. Diggs Jr.
> Member of Congress

International plane trips were challenging also because the average Black traveler didn't know where he would be welcome, what immunizations were necessary, or how and when to exchange currency. These were things only elite professionals and celebrities knew. Victor Green's Reservation Bureau helped Black travelers with some of these logistics, but it was the Henderson Travel Agency that specialized in assisting Black Americans who wanted to travel internationally. It was opened in 1954 by a Black woman named

Freddye Henderson, and it was the first fully accredited Black travel agency in America.

Henderson was the first Black person to receive a master's degree in fashion merchandising from New York University, and she went on to teach fashion and textiles at Spelman College. While attending a fashion show in Europe in 1954, she got the idea that if Black people knew how much better they were treated abroad, they would travel overseas. So when she returned to the States, she started the Henderson Travel Service with her husband, Jacob.

Shirley Coleman, the Hendersons' daughter, remembers that her parents "eventually took thousands of people across the world." During the early 1950s, travel to Africa wasn't easy for anyone, and Henderson's was one of only a handful of agencies that offered services there. Pan Am was the only U.S. air carrier that offered regular service to that continent, but most of these flights served white American game hunters and those taking safaris in East Africa. Henderson chartered planes to West Africa, an area of the continent where there were no commercial flights.

Coleman continues: "When my parents first started, white people were going [to Africa] for hunting or safari. Nobody was going for the culture. Nobody valued the culture. They didn't even know about the culture. It was a 'Dark Continent,' and so my parents, through their agency, helped to show people it's not just dark . . . [T]he people are colorful, the culture is rich."

Henderson also wrote a syndicated weekly column, "Travel by Freddye," which ran in the *Pittsburgh Courier* from 1957 to 1963. She was very popular, and it wasn't long before she was planning Martin Luther King Jr.'s trip to Oslo to accept his Nobel Peace Prize. But Henderson didn't only plan the journey; she accompanied King to Norway to accept the prize!

Victor Green's Reservation Bureau also organized itineraries to Africa, but the *Green Book* didn't have listings in that continent until the 1963–64 edition, which featured thirty African countries, including Algeria, Cameroon, Chad, the Congo, Ethiopia, Ghana, the Ivory Coast (Cote d'Ivoire), Liberia, Libya, Mali, Morocco, Nigeria, Rwanda, Senegal, Somalia, Sudan, and Uganda.

Green's affinity for Africa was evident when he published a full-page ad, on the inside cover of the 1952 edition, for African artifacts, including hand-carved Nigerian ebony shoehorns, knives, animal figurines, and native headpieces. Having this advertisement be the first thing his readers saw spoke volumes about Green's desire to broaden the definition of travel for them.

At the end of the 1952 and 1953 editions, Green published a "Vacation" section, listing resorts, beaches, lodges, and farmhouse hotels. Placed after the regular state-by-state listings, it was brief, at only six pages long. Some states had just one or two listings, and not all the states were covered. The section highlighted seasonal businesses serving summer travelers in remote coastal areas and on islands and peninsulas, and included Cape Cod, Martha's Vineyard, and beaches along the Atlantic coast.

Green had listed Jones Beach, in Long Island, and a handful of others in the late 1930s, but it wasn't until 1950 that any other beaches made it into the *Green Book*. Most beaches were staunchly segregated, and over the life of the guide, only seven were included. Two of the most popular were

's advertise

Hoppy Adams and performers at Carr's Beach

Carr's and Sparrow's Beach, both on the Chesapeake Bay, near Annapolis, Maryland, just thirty-three miles from Washington, DC. In 1959 this part of Maryland was still segregated, but these beaches were integrated. Carr's was originally purchased by Frederick Carr, a former slave, but eventually both it and Sparrow's Beach were run by his daughters, Elizabeth Carr Smith and Florence Carr Sparrow. Florence had inherited the land and turned it into a beach resort in the early 1930s. She also developed Sparrow's Beach nearby, and built cabins for guests. The resorts hosted summer camps, church picnics, beauty contests, and dances. Also on-site were baseball fields, a Ferris wheel, concessions, and a pavilion for private parties. Sensational musical artists such as Billie Holiday, Count Basie, Ella Fitzgerald, Duke Ellington, Dinah Washington, James Brown, Chuck Berry, Fats Domino, Little Richard, Etta James, Ray Charles, and Aretha Franklin drew crowds of more than ten thousand people.

The few predominately white beaches that tolerated Black people didn't offer a pleasant, relaxing experience. In many cases, Black sunbathers weren't allowed to use the lockers, so they would have to either arrive in their swimsuits or change on the beach while family members held up towels for privacy. And if the whole family wanted to go into the water, they would have to leave their clothes on their blankets, all too often only to return to find that everything had been stolen.

Places such as South Carolina's Atlantic Beach served both Black and white people, but it was by no means integrated. The Black section of the beach, called the "Black Pearl," was founded by George W. Tyson, a Black businessman who had purchased forty-seven acres of oceanfront land in 1934. He sold parcels to Black vacationers until 1957. The Gullah Geechee community, made up of descendants of slaves, had lived along the South Carolina coastline for centuries and regularly visited this beach. In the 1940s and '50s, Atlantic Beach grew in popularity and became a major tourist destination.

White property owners along the northern and southern borders of Atlantic Beach made sure that Black beachgoers didn't cross over onto the white section by putting up signs, fences, walls, and brightly colored ropes. Dino Thompson remembers, "Atlantic Beach had a rope from the land across to the ocean . . . It was an orange rope, I think. And it went out about two hundred yards, so the Blacks were supposed to stop swimming at the rope."

Unlike the clear demarcation of "Colored" or "White" for water fountains, segregating a body of water was an imprecise procedure and must have been frustrating and sometimes terrifying for Black vacationers just trying to have fun. Staying on the right side of the rope at segregated public beaches was critical, and there were consequences for those who didn't follow the rules.

As late as the early 1970s, Herbert Sulaiman remembers, "If a Black person was walking down there [Myrtle Beach,] and [if] they didn't have a card saying they worked at such-and-such, they could be arrested. They

would be harassed. If you didn't have the *Green Book* and if a Black person is going up to Atlantic Beach and they got a little bit confused and went to the wrong place, they could have gotten hurt. You ran into a lot of problems. And that's the way it was."

Maintaining racialized recreational spaces was an ongoing issue throughout the country. When seventeen-year-old Eugene Williams drifted into the unofficial "white" section of Lake Michigan, he was stoned by whites and drowned. This happened during the so-called "Red Summer" of 1919, when race riots broke out in more than three dozen cities. Williams's drowning incited the Chicago race riots that year, spawning a weeklong period of bloodshed. The *Chicago Tribune* called it the "deadliest episode of racial violence in Chicago history."

It was nearly twenty years after Williams's drowning that Jones, Rosedale, and Sparrow's Beaches were featured in the *Green Book*, and Carr's Beach wasn't listed until a decade after that. Still, this was a significant stride for the Black community, who finally were able to take a vacation and not worry about their safety.

Another popular Black resort that offered swimming, relaxation, and even an amusement park was in Idlewild, Michigan, one of the most legendary Black lakeside resorts in America. Located in a secluded rural area in northwestern Michigan about sixty miles from Grand Rapids, this "Black Eden," as it was called, was popular with Black celebrities of all kinds. W. E. B. Du Bois, Cab Calloway, Zora Neale Hurston, Langston Hughes, and

Women vacationing at Carr's Beach, 1956

Madam C. J. Walker went there to frolic, fish, swim, camp, roller-skate, and ride horses. With its carnival-themed atmosphere, skating rink, clubhouse, and amusement park, Idlewild became a favorite place for affluent Black families to play.

Idlewild had been purchased in 1912 by four white land developers, but it was marketed exclusively to Black people, making it one of the few places where they could buy a vacation home. It was the largest resort of its kind, spanning nearly three thousand acres. During its heyday, more than twenty-five thousand people patronized its more than three hundred Black-owned businesses. Ten of them were listed in the *Green Book* from 1938 to 1967. The mother of Loretta Long, an African American voice artist most famous for

Vacationing at Idlewild, Michigan, 1938

playing Susan on *Sesame Street*, ran the Hickory Inn, which was listed in the *Green Book*. Tourists and residents could see Etta James, Dinah Washington, and Aretha Franklin perform at Idlewild's Paradise Club, another *Green Book* listing. After that, partygoers could head over to Club El Morocco, a *Green Book* site that didn't even open until two a.m. and stayed in operation until the wee hours of the morning.

Another popular *Green Book* vacation site was Shearer Cottage, in Oak Bluffs, on Martha's Vineyard, a family-owned business that opened in 1903. The owner, Charles Shearer, who was born a slave, turned this cottage into the first inn for Black vacationers on the Vineyard. Like Idlewild, Shearer Cottage has a long, storied history, and it attracted the Black elite and intelligentsia. Artists, judges, lawyers, and celebrities such as Paul Robeson, Ethel Waters, and the Reverend Adam Clayton Powell Sr. all vacationed there; more recently, Lionel Richie and the Commodores vacationed there.

Most *Green Book* vacation resorts were located along the northern lakes and on the Eastern Seaboard. There were very few in the West, but the two most popular in California were Val Verde and Lake Elsinore. Val Verde offered horseback riding, hiking, swimming, and dancing. As for Lake Elsinore, located about ninety miles from Los Angeles, it was one of the most popular integrated vacation resorts at that time, offering stunning views of the Santa Ana Mountains, natural hot springs to soak in, and plenty of amenities, including a hotel, cabins, and a ranch. Six Lake Elsinore sites were included in the *Green Book*, including the Lake Elsinore Hotel, the largest hotel in the resort, complete with cottages, campgrounds, a croquet area, and a tennis court.

In addition to including its "Vacation" section, the 1952 *Green Book* had a long list of national parks supplied by the Department of the Interior. It was unusual to see national parks marketed to Black Americans. Although approximately fifty million vacationers visited national parks in the early 1950s, more than 90 percent of them were white. Moreover, national parks weren't a sought-after tourist destination for most Black people because the facilities were generally segregated, and "Colored" bathrooms were often poorly maintained and sometimes nonexistent.

Segregation had been an ongoing issue since the inception of the National Parks System. In 1922 a debate was held in Yosemite National Park to determine whether the national parks could exclude Black Americans. It was decided that "while colored people could not be openly discriminated against, they should be told that the parks have no facilities for taking care of them."

There were twenty-seven national parks listed in the 1952 edition of the *Green Book,* including Bryce Canyon, Crater Lake, Mesa Verde, Grand Canyon, Sequoia, Zion, and Yellowstone. There are no photographs of the parks in this article, just a list, along with one or two options for accommodation. Some parks, such as Big Bend, in Texas, list only one tourist home; the listing for Carlsbad Caverns simply states, "No overnight accommodations."

The Shenandoah National Park and the Great Smoky Mountains offered "Colored Campgrounds" with separate swimming and picnic areas. Park Service engineers and landscape architects had placed the Black campgrounds on the outer boundaries of the Great Smoky Mountains. While the park was being designed, more than four thousand men were hired to work as stewards, company clerks, and camp sergeants. When four Black men applied for a job there, the locals said it would be a "serious mistake" and that the men would probably be run out of the area. As a result, only white men worked in the camps.

Crater Lake Lodge, a former *Green Book* hotel located in Crater Lake National Park, Crater Lake, Oregon

Vacationing with "good old boys" lurking in the mountains was not relaxing or fun for Black Americans, and because most national parks are located in isolated rural areas, it's not surprising that Black people generally avoided these places federally designated as America's most scenic lands. It wasn't until the late 1950s that many of the national parks listed in the 1952 *Green Book* article featured hotels. These included the Ahwahnee, in Yosemite; the Bryce Canyon Lodge, in Utah; and the Crater Lake Lodge, in Oregon. (The number of Black people visiting national parks is still low today. A survey of national park visitors in 2016 revealed that only 7 percent of the attendees were Black.)

Some Black Americans avoid national parks because the woods can trigger historical trauma that has followed some families for generations. When Nina Roberts, an associate professor of recreation, parks, and tourism at San Francisco State University, asked a nineteen-year-old woman in a focus group why she avoided national parks, the woman said, "Why would I want to go? My granddaddy told me the KKK hangs out up in the mountains."

Her story likely rang true with many Black families.

For Black travelers who wanted to avoid wooded areas as vacation spots, the 1953 *Green Book* included the San Cristóbal Valley Ranch, a forty-acre ranch that celebrated diversity in a pastoral community north of Taos, New Mexico.

A white couple, Craig and Jenny Vincent, operated the ranch in the years it appeared in the *Green Book*. Soon after they married, the couple had turned San Cristóbal into a guest ranch, where they served Black travelers, supported Native American rights, and celebrated the rising Chicano movement.

Another rural *Green Book* site that was popular with the Black community was the Marsalis Mansion, located on the outskirts of New Orleans. It was run by Ellis Marsalis Sr., the grandfather of jazz musicians Wynton and Branford Marsalis. When Marsalis purchased the property, it was only a chicken coop surrounded by cows and mulberry trees, but he turned it into a forty-room hotel with plush-carpeted suites, color televisions, a restaurant, a lounge, and a pool. During the 1950s, the Marsalis Mansion became

The San Cristobal Academy was formerly the San Cristobal Ranch, a *Green Book* site in San Cristóbal, New Mexico.

a landing spot for musical artists such as Dinah Washington, Ray Charles, Ike and Tina Turner, and Etta James, and civil rights leaders Thurgood Marshall and Dr. Martin Luther King Jr.

The 1952 edition of the *Green Book* features a seven-page article on New Orleans that highlights the city's architecture, cuisine, and music. There is also a section dedicated to "Catholic Negroes in New Orleans," and to Xavier University, the only Black Catholic college in America.

Since New Orleans was segregated by law, there were no *Green Book* listings for sites in its popular French Quarter. The city's neighborhoods were redlined, and in some areas, Black people could enter the parks only on Wednesday, or "Negro Day." But the rolling, pristine manicured lawns of the

Black suburb Pontchartrain Park featured two hundred acres and one thousand homes. Although the neighborhood bordered a sprawling golf course designed by African American architect Joseph Bartholomew, Black people weren't permitted to use it.

The *Green Book* article on New Orleans is unlike most travel articles. Some of the piece covers the beautiful wrought iron balconies and quaint courtyards that could be found in the French Quarter, but it also highlights the importance of the levees in a city surrounded by swamps and sandwiched between the Mississippi River and Lake Pontchartrain. As long as the river wasn't flooding, it was a blessing, because the ports along the Mississippi provided stable employment for the city's residents. But since there were no Black-owned banks in New Orleans, Black men who worked along the Mississippi couldn't easily find a place to cash their checks. To solve that problem, many lined up outside Dooky Chase's Restaurant on Friday nights to cash checks and grab a bite to eat.

Dooky Chase's legendary restaurant opened in 1941, and was listed in the *Green Book* from 1947 to 1964. After Dooky's death, his wife, Leah Chase, ran the business for more than seventy years, until she passed away in 2019. It was her idea to transform Dooky Chase's from a bar and sandwich shop into a white tablecloth Creole restaurant, making it the first African American fine-dining establishment in the country. Her displays of African American art in the restaurant made it the first art gallery for Black artists in New Orleans. Leah's iconic status was confirmed when Disney modeled its first African American princess, Tiana, after her in the 2009 animated musical film *The Princess and the Frog*.

During the civil rights era, in a meeting room at Dooky's, Dr. Martin Luther King Jr., Thurgood Marshall, and members from the Student Nonviolent Coordinating Committee (SNCC) and the NAACP ate Creole food and strategized the most effective ways to fight racism.

For more than seventy years, Dooky Chase's has fed locals, tourists, celebrities, political powerhouses, and literary giants, including James Baldwin, the Reverend Jesse Jackson, and Quincy Jones. Leah also enjoyed serving President Barack Obama, but she admitted that when he tried to put hot sauce on her gumbo, she slapped his hand and reprimanded him just like she would have done anyone else.

Leah Chase in the kitchen at Dooky Chase's restaurant in New Orleans, Louisiana

The year the New Orleans article was featured in the *Green Book* was the same year Victor Green retired from the post office after being a letter carrier for thirty-nine years. From then on, he was free to work on his guide full time, which he did until his death in 1960. Thankfully, Green didn't face much opposition producing the guide. And why would he? For the most part,

Family traveling in a four-door sedan, 1950s

its users break any current laws. And given that 90 percent of the early editions featured Black-owned businesses, it was a win-win both for Black travelers who wanted to feel welcome and for those who preferred to keep Black people in Black spaces.

Still, although the *Green Book* was not a direct challenge to the established practices of racism and segregation, it had a profound and subversive effect. Whether Black people were traveling along the open highway, swimming at Carr's Beach, partying at Idlewild, or flying abroad for an adventure on the other side of the world, the *Green Book* gave them the courage to throw caution to the wind and take a vacation like everyone else.

Chapter 7
MUSIC VENUES

Blues, jazz, and R&B were the salve that softened the scars of Jim Crow and made everything seem better. Victor Green knew how important music was to his community, which is why there were more than 330 nightclubs listed in the *Green Book* during its lifetime.

The book was like a surrogate guide of Chitlin' Circuit venues. ("Chitlin'" is homage to a type of soul food.) The Chitlin' Circuit was a string of dozens of nightclubs, restaurants, and theaters where Black musicians knew they would

Jack's Chicken Basket, a *Green Book* nightclub in Los Angeles, California

Lenox Lounge advertisement in the *Green Book*, 1948

be welcome while touring the United States. Some of the most famous musicians never hit the road without the *Green Book*. For instance, Ella Fitzgerald was a regular at *Green Book* listings, including the Jim Hotel in Fort Worth, Texas; the Broadview Hotel in Omaha, Nebraska; Carr's Beach, near Annapolis, Maryland; the Dunbar in Los Angeles; the Rossonian in Denver; the Sunset in Indianapolis; and several nightclubs in San Francisco's Fillmore District.

Duke Ellington also performed, slept, and dined at the Sunset, Carr's Beach, the Dunbar, and the Rossonian. He was a regular at other *Green Book* sites, including Ma Sutton's restaurant in Atlanta; Carioca Hall in St. Louis, Missouri; the Idlewild resort in Michigan; Charlie's Place in Myrtle Beach, South Carolina; Hotel Theresa in Harlem; Hotel Terrace Hall in Pittsburgh's Hill District; the Hampton House in Miami; and the Astor Motel in Jacksonville, Florida.

Some of the most famous nightclubs in the *Green Book* were in Harlem in New York City. Club 845 was one of the most important venues for jazz, especially bebop. Thelonious Monk, Dexter Gordon, Charlie Parker, and Sonny Rollins all played there in the late forties and early fifties.

Live music was performed nightly in Harlem's Lenox Lounge, also listed in the *Green Book*. At the Lenox, patrons sat in plush leather booths beneath zebra-print papered walls to hear swing, bebop, and the modern, profound, and transcendental artistry of John Coltrane and Miles Davis. Writers James Baldwin and Langston Hughes were regulars, and one of the booths was reserved for Billie Holiday.

North of the Lenox Lounge, the Savoy, a legendary *Green Book* nightclub, was always jumping with people dancing the Lindy Hop, the Rhumboogie, the jitterbug, the snakehips, the shimmy, and the mambo. A huge space stretching an entire block, the Savoy, which opened in 1926, was one of the first integrated clubs in Harlem. Actress Lana Turner called it the "Home of Happy Feet," and each year, nearly seven hundred thousand people danced in its ten-thousand-square-foot pink ballroom lined with mirrored walls. Two bandstands hosted the best performers at the height of their careers, including Benny Goodman, Thelonious Monk, and Charlie Parker. The crowds just couldn't get enough, especially when Ella Fitzgerald hit the stage.

New York City had nearly sixty music venues listed in the *Green Book*. And the music didn't stop there. Not only did Victor Green celebrate live music venues, he also brought attention to radio disc jockeys when he published an article in the 1955 edition dedicated to popular radio personality "Big Joe" (born Joe Rosenfield), who deejayed on WMGM. Big Joe's radio program, *Happiness Exchange*, spread cheer from midnight to two a.m. Although the show aired from New York City, people tuned in from as far north as Canada, as far south as Florida, and as far west as the Mississippi River.

Although most radio stations, like the one where Rosenfield worked, were white-owned, by 1955 "personality deejays" were wildly popular, and there were about six hundred Black radio stations on the air. It wasn't just the music they played, but also their smooth voices and ad-libbed charm that drew listeners in.

Black-owned nightclubs, such as Jack's Basket Room (also known as Jack's Chicken Basket), a jazz club that opened in the heart of South Central Los Angeles in 1939, also found a place in the *Green Book*. Owned by Jack Johnson, the first Black heavyweight boxing champion, the Basket Room hosted the nation's top entertainers and served the Black bourgeoisie. It was right down the street from the Dunbar Hotel, where celebrity musicians stayed. To relax, socialize, and have fun while they were in town, they went up the street to Jack's.

Jack's in-house radio station, KXLA, featured deejay King Perry, the "Pied Piper of Swingdom." He and his sextet were broadcast three nights a week starting at 11:45 p.m. This was the first radio broadcasting station on Los Angeles's Eastside, and disc jockeys Bill Sampson and Nick Thomas spun vinyl (played music) in the radio booth until three a.m.

Jack's was known as "the place where everyone comes to play." Cab Calloway's lyrics "A chicken ain't nothin' but a bird" were painted on the outside of the building. Inside, chicken, steaks, ham, bacon, and barbecue were dished out until two a.m., and the music lasted until dawn.

Being at Jack's was an all-night affair. A typical Monday night jam session featured trumpeter Howard McGhee and Sammy Franklin and his Atomics. Female impersonators also entertained crowds with two floor shows between 12:30 a.m. and 3:15 a.m. Night owls would stay for the breakfast dance at six a.m.

Jack's Chicken Basket, a *Green Book* nightclub in Los Angeles, California

Jack's Basket Room also hosted Sunday afternoon matinees of music and other entertainment, and held an annual Christmas dinner for underprivileged children, serving up to a thousand free turkey dinners with all the trimmings and ice cream for dessert.

Disc jockey Bill Sampson in the radio booth at Jack's Chicken Basket in Los Angeles, California, 1949

Los Angeles had seventeen nightclubs listed in the *Green Book*, but Black people who traveled as far west as the Pacific Ocean could also find a thriving and phenomenal jazz scene in San Francisco's Fillmore District. Black people had been living in the Fillmore District, a multiethnic neighborhood, since the turn of the twentieth century, and it was a mecca for Black musicians. But things changed in 1941 when approximately five thousand Japanese American residents of the Fillmore District were rounded up and forced to live in internment camps after Japan bombed Pearl Harbor, launching the United States into World War II. Most had been born in the United States but were incarcerated simply because of their ancestry. These men, women, and children, forced to live in horrific conditions, lost almost everything if not everything.

As the years passed the Fillmore became a primarily Black neighborhood. During the war Black people migrated to the district to work for the defense industry in the Bay Area. By the time the 1954 *Green Book* was published, San Francisco's Black population had risen from just under five thousand before World War II to nearly forty-five thousand people.

Racism wasn't as flagrant in San Francisco as it was in the surrounding sundown towns of Burlingame and San Leandro. Although the *Green Book* celebrated neighboring Berkeley for its "casual acceptance of people regardless of their race, creed, or color," it also admitted that about 35 percent of San Francisco's Black residents were unemployed, and that "comfortable housing" and "business opportunities" for them were limited.

Surprisingly, one of the neighborhood's most iconic music theaters, The Fillmore (formerly Majestic Hall), wasn't listed in the *Green Book*, but other seminal music sites were, such as Club Alabam, the Town Club, and Jack's Tavern, the first club in the area to cater to Black people. R&B singer Sugar Pie DeSanto remembers when she and her cousin Etta James would go to the clubs in the Fillmore District. "It was like a little Vegas . . . Thelonious Monk, Nancy Wilson, any famous person could walk in and get up on stage and jam . . . Everyone would get dressed up in those days . . . and there were no fights. The crowd was mixed, and for a while, the police didn't like it. They hassled us for a little while, but . . . we told the cops to leave us alone. We didn't care about color. We cared about music."

Music brought Black and white communities together in the South as well. Dino Thompson, who grew up in Myrtle Beach, South Carolina, remembers a legendary *Green Book* nightclub, Charlie's Place (also listed as "Fitzgerald's"). Some of the greatest stars performed there, including Etta James, Fats Domino, Billie Holiday, Count Basie, and James Brown. Dino, a white man, started going to Charlie's Place when he was just a teenager. He loved to dance, and the music at Charlie's was unlike anything he had ever heard. "They had something that we didn't have," he remembers. "The greatest Black music on earth, and it was something we all wanted."

People went to Charlie's Place to dance to beats white people in the area had never heard. As Dino said, Charlie's Place featured music that was "not allowed to be played on your jukebox or on your radio in Tennessee, West Virginia, or Ohio . . . But you could go to Charlie's Place [or] Atlantic Beach, and it was wafting out of every patio."

The music played at Charlie's was called "beach music." It was so popular that once record executives learned about it, they wanted in on the craze. Jerry Wexler, the president of Atlantic Records, put out six or seven beach music songs every three weeks and marketed them to the Black community. When he noticed that white teenagers were ordering these records by the thousands, he couldn't understand it, as they hadn't been the target market. So he sent songwriter Jesse Stone (who had written "Shake Rattle and Roll" under the pseudonym "Charles E. Calhoun") to see what was going on in Myrtle Beach. Stone reported back that the locals were doing the jitterbug and a dance called "the shag," and that they'd buy anything that, unlike white music, had a danceable backbeat. Stone told Wexler, "They're dancing all over the place down there."

Dancers at integrated club, circa 1950s

When Dino heard that Little Richard was going to perform at Charlie's Place, he was beside himself. At the time, Little Richard was one of the biggest acts in the world. As Dino remembers, "The place was packed. [Charlie] put me at the end of the stage, and Little Richard's dancing all over me. I remember he had blue suede shoes with metal buckles, metal fronts, and metal backs; I'd never seen a pair of shoes like that. He did his thing, 'Tutti Frutti,' 'Long Tall Sally' . . . Afterward, Charlie had somebody walk me back to my dad's diner. It's like twelve thirty a.m. now. I told Dad I'd seen Little Richard, and he was playing the piano with his head and his elbows and his feet, and my dad blew smoke up in the air and said, 'What's the matter with the man? He's got no hands?' I didn't bother to explain. I just said, 'Well, you shoulda seen it.'"

Charlie Fitzgerald registered to vote in 1948, becoming one of the first African Americans in Myrtle Beach to do so since Reconstruction. He owned a twenty-two-unit motel called the Whispering Pines, an adjoining restaurant, and a cab company. Charlie had stature and power, economic power, and that meant something in Myrtle Beach.

Charlie's success entitled him to respect, and for the most part, no one bothered him. He went where he wanted, ate next to white people at Dino's parents' Kozy Korner diner, and sat in the white section of the Broadway Theater. The local Black kids, who were told to stay away from the white section of town, would run up to the Kozy Korner anyhow and peek through the window just to look at Charlie sitting there, big as day, eating with white people. To them, he was like a rock star.

But Charlie was prepared if someone caused trouble. Dino recalls that he always saw him wearing a coat or a suit that concealed a pearl-handled revolver. He called it "my just-in-case."

Dino says, "Charlie, for some reason, didn't allow himself to be discriminated against." Dino remembers walking by a "Colored" water fountain with Charlie. "I asked, 'Mr. Charlie, do you drink out of that "Colored" water fountain?' Charlie said nonchalantly, 'Never noticed it.'"

That was the kind of man Charlie was. Cool, calm, and confident. To him, Jim Crow signs were merely a suggestion. But a Black man with this much capital and social power did not sit well with the Ku Klux Klan. And on August 26, 1950, everything changed.

It was a Saturday night, and Charlie's Place was hopping. There were probably close to a hundred people jitterbugging and dancing the shag. Down the street, Dino's mother cried as she stood in the window of the Kozy Korner and watched a caravan of sixteen or seventeen (some people reported seeing twenty-six) carfuls of hooded Ku Klux Klan members driving down Carver Street displaying shoulder rifles. The "grand dragon" of the Klan led the procession in a Continental with a siren and a four-foot-tall iron cross lit up with red lightbulbs welded to the front bumper. The Klan members got out of their cars and walked up Carver Street to Charlie's Place and then continued onto Atlantic Beach. Their mere presence terrorized the community.

After seeing the Klan pass his nightclub, Charlie called the sheriff and predicted that if the Klan came back to his place, there might be trouble. Somehow the story got back to the Klan, and they took it as a dare. They turned around and drove back to Charlie's Place. A short, heavy Klansman with a banner around his neck got out of

Charlie and Sara Fitzgerald

the lead car and yelled to about sixty of his brethren, "Get your guns ready, and everybody get in line!" They stood outside Charlie's Place and, at point-blank range, pummeled about four hundred rounds of ammunition into it.

The shooting happened just before midnight. Black and white patrons of Charlie's bolted out the back. Several were injured, but by some miracle, the only person who was killed was a Klansman, an off-duty police officer from the neighboring town of Conway, South Carolina.

Charlie remained at the scene. He recognized a large man as the owner of the Shell gas station, who told the group, "This is Charlie; he's the one we want." Before he could turn around, Charlie was knocked out cold. They took his gun, threw him in the trunk of a car, drove around for an hour and a half, and then took him deep into the woods, where they tied him to a tree and tortured him. The FBI report noted that the grand dragon of the KKK said they cut off his earlobes to "mark him, so we'll know him."

Somehow Charlie escaped and was rescued on Highway 544. Sheriff C. Ernest Sasser put him in three jails over a two-week period to "protect" him from the Klan. After that, Charlie disappeared for a while. While he was away, his wife Sara Fitzgerald, continued to run the businesses.

Dino remembers, years later, seeing Charlie come into the Kozy Korner; he had no earlobes. Dino said, "[T]hey sat down—a couple of Greeks, a couple of Jews, an Italian, Charlie, and my dad. Had a beer. Life went on. And they never spoke about it again."

In 1956, six years after Charlie's Place was shot up by the Klan, the *Green Book* published a spring and a fall edition to commemorate its twenty-year anniversary. The spring edition hit the stands with a brand-new layout and design. The most noticeable change was that the standard two columns had been replaced with a single-column format. Accommodations were still listed alphabetically by state and city, but the types of listings were limited to lodging and restaurants. From 1938 to 1955 the *Green Book*s had been filled with juke joints and nightclubs that hosted some of the best jazz and blues players of the twentieth century. Now, with the 1956 edition, the music venues (along with gas stations, drugstores, tailors, hair salons, liquor stores, sanitariums, and haberdashers) were all gone. Some nightclubs reappeared in the last two editions, but they were no longer a regular category listed under each major city.

This new version of the *Green Book* functioned more like an AAA guide (American Automobile Association, the travel agency founded by motor clubs), with the number of listings from the previous editions slashed in half. The 1955 and the 1956 editions were roughly eighty pages and averaged sixty-five sites per page, but the layout in the 1956 edition had only about thirty listings on each page.

This radical redesign of the *Green Book* happened right after the Supreme Court's *Brown v. Board of Education* decision, in which 755 school districts were under an immediate, mandatory order to desegregate. Things didn't go smoothly, and there was an enormous backlash, but the fact that the law had changed must have contributed to Victor Green's feelings toward the state of integration and racial progress in America.

By necessity, earlier *Green Book* editions had listed businesses outside what would typically have been found in traditional travel guides because Black Americans were legally shut out of nearly every segment of society. It's unknown why the change was made, but by no longer including barbershops, drugstores, service stations, and taverns, it's possible that Green felt the tide of racial segregation was subsiding—still, this radical shift in listings was a significant loss.

Regardless of the change, the *Green Book* still saved lives and helped preserve the dignity of Black Americans. Dino Thompson summed it up when he said of the *Green Book*, "[It] didn't tell you if a place had a good steak, or good seafood, or had a soft bed . . . it told you where you would be safe; it told you where you'd be welcome."

Chapter 8

THE ROOTS OF ROUTE 66

The freeway on-ramp that graces the cover of the 1957 *Green Book* is not particularly interesting, but it's significant because the Federal Aid Highway Act had been signed into law by President Dwight D. Eisenhower in 1956. Twenty-six billion dollars was spent to construct a forty-one-thousand-mile network of interstate highways to make U.S. travel safer and more efficient.

In the late 1950s, Americans both Black and white loved their cars, and

Green Book cover, 1957

1957 Edition

$1.25

The Negro Travelers'

Green Book

THE GUIDE FOR TRAVEL AND VACATIONS
20 Years of Service to the Negro Traveler

Carry your GREEN BOOK with you—you may need it.

automobile ownership increased throughout the country. *Ebony* magazine estimated that 20 percent of Black households intended to buy a new car in 1958. Freeways offered a new and exciting driving experience. These smoothly curved ribbons of concrete etched into the landscape made Americans want to drive even more.

Coasting on a freeway was a powerful new experience. As the road soared into the distance, it seemed to go on forever, with no obstacles, and no pockmarked surfaces. With passengers engaged in a song or a story, the hours flew by, and all the while, the beauty of the land, the sky, and the road were framed in the window as chrome-finned cars sliced through the wind like rockets. Before the Highway Act, taking a road trip involved driving on county and farm roads, and motorists had to pass through small towns on Main Streets across America. The freeways transformed the entire experience. Drivers could now bypass stop signs, traffic signals, and railroad crossings.

But before the interstate highways spanned the country, there was one particular road that symbolized freedom, prosperity, and the pursuit of the American Dream: Route 66. Like an artery, the "Mother Road," as many called it, nurtured communities and serviced millions.

The 2,448-mile highway connecting urban and rural America from Chicago to Los Angeles crossed eight states and three time zones and passed through practically every type of landscape the country had to offer—from the gritty metropolis of downtown Chicago, past Missouri trailer parks and churches, and on to Texas's towering grain silos and stockyards. It bisected the Texas Panhandle to Oklahoma's windswept plains, passed New Mexico's ancient pueblos, soared around hairpin curves hugging Arizona's Black

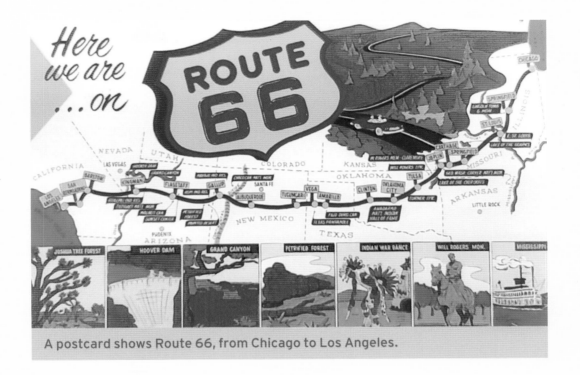

A postcard shows Route 66, from Chicago to Los Angeles.

Mountain, and descended into California's Mojave Desert, where it then headed dead west through the Inland Empire and on to the traffic-choked streets of downtown Los Angeles.

Gas stations, motels, and diners dished out hospitality on Route 66. With few resources, Americans motored west on this "road of dreams," which symbolized a pathway to easier times. It was one of the few U.S. highways laid out diagonally, and it sliced across the country like a shortcut to freedom.

Whether you were driving west to escape poverty or just on vacation, the experience of driving Route 66 was not the same for everyone. When the *Green Book* was first published, roughly half of the eighty-nine counties on Route 66 were sundown counties. By the 1950s, about 35 percent of the counties on Route 66 didn't allow Black motorists after six p.m. And although the road was open to Black travelers, it was unknown where they could find a meal or a place to rest because six of the eight states that lined the Mother Road as far west as Arizona had segregation laws.

Since every county enforced its segregation laws differently, Black motorists had no idea what to expect as they drove on Route 66. Missouri and Illinois were the worst states, with the highest percentage of sundown towns. Even California, a state that had the lowest number of sundown towns and no formal segregation laws on the books, segregated its beaches. Moreover, Los Angeles was surrounded by the sundown suburbs of Burbank, Glendale, and Culver City.

Construction on Route 66 began in 1926, a decade before the *Green Book* was first published, and during the life of the guide, the road underwent three major realignments. Sometimes the decision to move the route was political. For example, a commissioner in a small town would reroute it to pass in front of favored local businesses. Some cities that were on the original alignment, such as Santa Fe, were later bypassed. Even the ending point was moved, from downtown Los Angeles to the Santa Monica Pier, which dead-ends into the Pacific Ocean. Much of the original 1926 alignment was built alongside the Santa Fe railroad tracks. In some states, such as New Mexico, the road was later moved hundreds of miles from the original route; in other places, it moved less than one-eighth of a mile away. The first realignment happened in 1937, one year after the *Green Book* was first published. After the 1945 realignment, some of the original 1926 route was taken over by weeds, and parts still had pavement that just abruptly stopped. These realignments made it easy for motorists to get lost, and even harder for them to find safe places to sleep or eat along the way.

The reality Black motorists had to accept when traveling along Route 66 was that there was virtually no way for them to know what was coming up around the bend. And there was no such thing as a list of sundown towns to assist them in planning their itinerary. We know about sundown towns today only because of Harvard sociologist James Loewen's recent research and scholarship. Loewen identified these all-white communities in retrospect by analyzing U.S. Census records. Before his work, the only warnings about places for Black motorists to avoid usually came from family members and friends.

When Earl Hutchinson left Chicago in the late 1950s and headed west on Route 66, it was the third time he'd left his home "in search of a promised land free of the burden of discrimination." It was clear his experience would be different from white motorists. "You knew that you couldn't eat in a roadside café or stay overnight at the roadside motel . . . [but we] grabbed *Green Book*."

Imperial Hotel, Pontiac, Ill.

The Imperial Hotel in Pontiac, Illinois , did not welcome Black travelers.

Just a few miles from Chicago were the sundown suburbs of Cicero, Berwyn, and Oak Park. Black motorists had to drive nearly two hundred miles to Springfield, Illinois, to find *Green Book* accommodations. On their way there, they had to travel about thirty miles southwest of Cicero to Joliet, which was overwhelmingly white and home to the second-largest steel mill in the United States. About forty miles from Joliet was the sundown town of Dwight, and another forty miles west from there was Lexington, another sundown town.

The town of Pontiac sat between Dwight and Lexington. It was a quaint Illinois town straight out of a Norman Rockwell painting that was filled with eighteenth-century brick buildings, beautiful parks, and tree-lined streets. Pontiac wasn't a sundown town, but the local movie theater was segregated, and Black people weren't allowed in the lobbies of the Imperial and Pontiac Hotels unless they were there to clean them.

Cansler's Lounge, Springfield, Illinois

Normal, Illinois, about thirty-five miles from Pontiac, had segregated and whites-only barbershops. When Charles Burton, the vice president of the NAACP chapter at the Illinois State University at Normal, went into a local barbershop, the barber told him he didn't have the tools to cut his hair.

In 1947 Black and white Americans picketed the Pilgrim Café, located near the Illinois State University campus in Normal, and they were eventually successful at desegregating the restaurant, but segregation was still enforced in other places. Robert Gaston remembers, "I can tell you that back in the fifties and sixties . . . you couldn't eat in a restaurant out there anywhere. You could get . . . a sandwich in a sack and walk down the street with it. But you couldn't eat out there anywhere."

The next major city, Springfield, Illinois, sits about sixty miles from Normal. Thankfully, it had twenty-six accommodations listed in the *Green Book*, including fourteen tourist homes (one operated by a Black doctor), three beauty parlors, one barbershop, two service stations, a drugstore, a hotel, and four taverns.

The next Route 66 state, Missouri, had a centuries-long history of overt racism entrenched in its social and legal practices. There were at least two hundred sundown towns in the state, and in 1943 the state legislature killed a bill that would have allowed Black people to go to its theaters and restaurants.

Joe Sonderman remembers, "Man, those rural areas [of Missouri] were just hell, [for Blacks] . . . They knew they had better pack lunch and bring a spare tire. A lot of the gasoline chains didn't serve African Americans; Esso was one of the only ones who went out of their way to help them. In rural areas every time you stopped, it was a chance for an encounter with a local that wouldn't go well. And even in parts of Missouri today [in 2015], there's a tremendous amount of that. I see it. There are places in St. Louis that you don't go if you are Black. And I'm not sure if we will ever be colorblind."

For Black travelers, it was best to get through Missouri as quickly as possible, without going over the speed limit, of course. Black motorists on Route 66 entered Missouri in St. Louis, which thankfully hosted plenty of *Green Book* accommodations.

Route 66 passed just a couple of miles north of Ferguson, a St. Louis suburb. Ferguson was a sundown town until the mid-1960s. After that the only Black people welcome in Ferguson were domestics and nannies, but because it was a sundown town, they were not allowed to stay overnight.

Seventy miles west of Ferguson, Route 66 motorists had to be careful in the sundown town of Sullivan, Missouri. Today Sullivan has approximately seven thousand residents and is believed to be a modern-day sundown town. It isn't 100 percent white, but it has held on to its white supremacist roots. Stefan Wehmeyer, a mixed-race man, went to high school in Sullivan and is one of a handful of Black people who still live there. In an article published in the *Guardian* in 2018, Wehmeyer spoke about what it's like to live in Sullivan. His next-door neighbor told Stefan's mother, "If your son ever goes on my property I'll kill him . . . I don't like niggers on my property." At school, Stefan's classmates dressed up in blackface and talked about going "coon hunting." And when he was called a "stupid nigger" at school, his teacher assured him that the N-word was a "term of endearment." How Wehmeyer learned in such a hostile environment is a mystery. He couldn't even find a safe place to sit in school. When he sat next to a white classmate, he was told,

"You need to move seats—if my dad finds me sitting with a nigger he'll beat us both up." Given that Wehmeyer was experiencing this in 2010, we can assume Black motorists in the 1950s didn't stop in Sullivan.

Once Black motorists passed through Sullivan they had to drive another one hundred and fifty miles to Springfield, Missouri, to find services listed in the *Green Book*. One of the most memorable was Alberta's Hotel, listed in the *Green Book* from 1954 to 1967.

Shortly after World War II, with the help of her family members, Alberta Ellis purchased a defunct hospital at auction for ten thousand dollars. (The hospital was supposed to have gone to a wealthy white man, but no one expected Alberta to show up to the auction with cash.) She turned the hospital into a hotel,

Alberta's Hotel, Springfield, Missouri

beauty salon, barbershop, and a nightclub called the Rumpus Room. One year before Alberta's appeared in the *Green Book*, Ellis purchased ten acres of land just west of the city to grow produce for the hotel's restaurant. A bed-and-breakfast on-site provided additional lodging when the hotel was fully booked.

Alberta's was a family-run operation that served everyone, from Route 66 motorists to celebrities passing through. The Drifters, a teenage Stevie Wonder, the Imperials, and the Harlem Globetrotters could be spotted there any day of the week. Alberta's sisters cooked, managed room service, and took care of the laundry while her husband watched over the place.

It's likely Black Missouri residents weren't surprised by 2017's NAACP-led Missouri travel ban that said Black people should exercise extreme caution when traveling there. This was no doubt especially true for those who live near the Ozarks, in the southern part of the state. Driving through the Ozarks has never been safe for Black people, and when the *Green Book* was published, the threat of physical violence and even lynching was real.

Klan meeting at Fantastic Caverns, Springfield, Missouri, 1920s

With no Internet or Black Twitter, Black motorists on Route 66 had no way of knowing that they should avoid a tourist site called Fantastic Caverns, in Springfield. It was advertised as a fun, kitschy drive-through cave, but it was run by the Ku Klux Klan, and they held their cross burnings inside. Fantastic Caverns is still open today, but the Klan no longer runs it.

It was places such as Fantastic Caverns that made every mile of Route 66 feel less like a fun adventure for Black travelers and more like a minefield. Also, since the route crossed two-thirds of the continent, motorists were bound to run into any kind of weather. Chicago has the most brutal, bitterly cold winters in the country, and in the fall, Oklahoma can be windier and colder than Chicago. Summer in Illinois, Missouri, and Kansas can be oppressively humid, and temperatures can reach over a hundred degrees in Texas, Arizona, New Mexico, and California's Mojave Desert.

From Springfield, Missouri, it was another fifty miles along Route 66 to find the nearest *Green Book* hotel, in the town of Carthage, Missouri. And there was only one option: Hap's. But thankfully, fifteen miles away, the town of Joplin had a hotel and five tourist homes.

Once Black motorists left Carthage, they drove thirteen miles along Route 66 through the southeastern corner of Kansas and then dipped into Oklahoma, which was notorious for Klan activity. Approximately seventy miles west of the Oklahoma border, Black motorists likely avoided the Grand Café in Claremore, with its EAT NIGGER CHICKEN sign displayed on the turnpike outside Vinita, Oklahoma.

From Joplin it was about one hundred miles to Tulsa, which had forty-two *Green Book* sites listed over the life of the guide. The majority of these were in Tulsa's Greenwood District, a vibrant Black community that happened to also be the site of one of the most devastating acts of terrorism on U.S. soil.

Between the turn of the twentieth century and 1921, the Greenwood District was a wealthy Black neighborhood with more than six hundred Black businesses. It was home to Black physicians, surgeons, lawyers, oil barons, and entrepreneurs. Black residents could patronize thirty restaurants and forty-one grocery stores. Greenwood also had Black libraries, parks, churches, hospitals, schools, construction companies, six real estate offices, and a Black bus line. Some Black residents were millionaires, and some owned private airplanes. Even the bellhops and young shoeshines could

Greenwood District ablaze,
Tulsa, Oklahoma

count on receiving about ten dollars a day in tips. This was significant, as their salaries were only about five dollars a week. There was so much wealth in the community, and the neighborhood was so prosperous, that Booker T. Washington gave Greenwood District the nickname "Black Wall Street."

Everything changed for the Greenwood District in 1921, when a riot broke out. It started as many race riots do: A young Black man was wrongly accused of a crime—this time assaulting a white woman. Once the word spread, a white mob crossed the railroad tracks into Greenwood and looted the businesses there. In less than twenty-four hours, three hundred people were dead and thirty-five square blocks of Black homes and Black businesses had been burned to the ground, leaving ten thousand Black residents homeless.

Ruins after the massacre, Tulsa, Oklahoma, June 1921

It's no question that long-held resentment from whites fueled the hatred. Amid the smoking embers, the message was loud and clear that if Black people achieved too much success, white people would find a way to destroy it.

The Greenwood District was rebuilt, but it never fully recovered from the events of that June day in 1921. The riot predated the *Green Book*, but out of the forty-two *Green Book* listings in Tulsa, the majority of them were in Greenwood.

In the 1950s Greenwood was still a major tourist destination for Black travelers, and one they were proud to visit. The Small Hotel, a *Green Book* site, hosted Louis Armstrong and the swing bandleader Walter Barnes. "I stopped with my entire orchestra at the modern and exclusive Small Hotel in Tulsa," Barnes said, "one of the best equipped in the country having newest electrical fixtures, telephone in each room, bath in every room, and modernistic furniture."

Threatt Filling Station, Luther, Oklahoma

The Threatt Filling Station in Luther, Oklahoma, served customers for nearly fifty years.

About seventy-five miles west of Tulsa, Black motorists could fuel up at the Threatt Filling Station, in Luther, Oklahoma, before passing through the sundown town of Edmond, Oklahoma. Threatt wasn't listed in the *Green Book*, but this Black family-owned gas station served Route 66 motorists from 1915 to the 1950s. The family had 160 acres of land and had built the gas station from the quarried sandstone on their property.

The station is no longer in operation, but the family still owns the sandstone bungalow there. Thankfully, the National Park Service has listed the Threatt Filling Station on its National Register of Historic Places, and the family hopes to reopen the station as a historic tourist site.

Alan Threatt Sr.'s son, Edmond, remembers having to deal with a litany of restrictions due to his race. Ironically, he was named after a neighboring sundown town, which didn't hide its hatred for Black people. A sign there read, DON'T LET THE SUN SET ON YOU IN THIS TOWN, and the town's Royce Café proudly announced on its postcards that Edmond was "A Good Place to Live. 6,000 Live Citizens. No Negroes."

About twenty miles west of Edmond, Oklahoma City was the next major Route 66 stop, with thirty-eight *Green Book* listings. In 1958 it was so segregated that a Black teacher of history, Clara Luper, led a sit-in at Katz Drug Store that lasted several weeks—eighteen months before the famous Greensboro lunch counter sit-ins. Luper's demonstrators sat at the lunch counter in the drugstore and refused to leave until their demands were met. Luper was arrested twenty-six times, but the sit-ins were so effective that over the following six years they led to the desegregation of nearly every restaurant in Oklahoma City.

"A Good Place to Live . . . No Negroes." Royce Café in Edmond, Oklahoma

Leaving Oklahoma, the farther west Black motorists drove on Route 66, the farther apart the cities with *Green Book* listings grew. For instance, from Oklahoma City, Route 66 motorists had to drive 260 miles, to Amarillo, Texas, where they would find thirty *Green Book* businesses. After leaving

Amarillo, there were no *Green Book* sites on Route 66 for another 110 miles, not until Tucumcari, New Mexico.

Once Black motorists crossed into New Mexico, there were only three cities over a three-hundred-fifty-mile stretch that had *Green Book* accommodations. Once they reached Albuquerque, only six out of the more than one hundred hotels that lined Central Avenue would rent a room to them. Folks who didn't have a *Green Book* would have had no idea which six motels those were. Many travelers were so exhausted from driving such long distances that by the time they reached Albuquerque they were getting into accidents. As reported in an *Albuquerque Tribune* article in August 1955, the state police chief determined that one accident that took six lives had been caused by "speed and fatigue." Edward L. Boyd, an NAACP official, said he wasn't surprised that six Black people had died due to fatigue. "They could not have found a welcome [sign] at any of the [motor] courts on Route 66 from the Texas border to Albuquerque," and the motels are "consistent in their refusal to accommodate Negroes."

No sleeping accommodations for this Black driver asleep under a truck, 1940

Leaving Albuquerque, Black motorists traveling Route 66 could next find rest 130 miles away, in Gallup, New Mexico. There were three lodging options in Gallup: a tourist home run by Mrs. Sonnie Lewis, the Casa Linda Motel, and the El Navajo Hotel.

From Gallup Black motorists had to drive 185 miles, to Flagstaff, to find the next *Green Book* sites. (Some Black travelers may have known that Harvey Houses served Black people, so they could have stopped at La Posada Hotel, in Winslow, Arizona, about 130 miles from Gallup.) Flagstaff didn't have any *Green Book* listings until 1957, but when it finally did, there were four lodging options. The Mountain Villa Motel in Kingman, Arizona (147 miles west of Flagstaff), was listed in the 1957 *Green Book*, and the White Rock Court appeared in the 1956 edition. These were the only listings for Kingman, but considering its status as a former sundown town, they were a blessing. After leaving Kingman, Route 66 climbed deep into the Black Hills.

Most Black families survived because they were prepared, traveling with ample food and camping along the way. Still it's unlikely they knew how treacherous the trip would be once they reached the Black Hills. In this stretch of Route 66, the two-lane road is narrow with sharp hairpin curves hugging the mountain on the south side and with sheer cliffs dropping off just a few feet from the edge of a car's tires. Driving through the Black Hills even during the day would have been nerve-wracking, but it would have been nothing compared to the harrowing trip if it was night and they were tired. There was nowhere to pull over to rest on the hairpin turns, and once they made it to the Mojave Desert, camping was a life-threatening ordeal. The desert brought searing daytime heat, and the temperature could drop to freezing at night. They also had to worry about sidewinders, scorpions, rattle-snakes, and black widow spiders crawling into their camp. The safest option was to just keep going.

Driving in the southwestern United States was especially challenging for Black motorists because they had to travel through triple-digit desert heat, and the threat of car trouble was always looming. If the car overheated, it was unlikely they would find help, as most of the towns didn't offer tow service for Black people. If they found themselves stranded on the side of the road, they had to pray that someone would give them a ride. It was also doubtful that they would find assistance from other Black people, as the Black residents had the lowest population statistics in the area, after whites, Mexicans, and Native Americans.

The first *Green Book* site a Black motorist could find in California was Murray's Dude Ranch, near Victorville, a forty-acre property on the edge of the Mojave Desert. Victorville was a sundown town, but Black homesteaders who settled near Bell Mountain, which bordered Victorville, had been there since the early twentieth century. Murray's was billed as "the only Negro Dude Ranch in the world"—and it very likely was, since Black people were banned from most dude ranches. Thankfully, Murray's offered Black Route 66 travelers much-needed lodging, food, and some good old-fashioned western recreation.

Murray's was owned by a Black couple, Nolie and Lela Murray. Lela dreamed of opening the property to troubled youth. She knew that the solitude and peace of the desert would provide comfort to inner-city children, who suffered from fear, stress, and poverty. Some children were sent to the ranch by the courts, some came to heal their asthma, and others came to relax, swim, and learn how to ride horses. By 1937 the Murrays had turned the property into a dude ranch, offering Black travelers a rare and unusual opportunity to experience the Old West. One man wrote to the Murrays, "I am a bachelor. I like to ride horseback very much. I have always wanted to spend a few weeks on a dude ranch. Being colored, I doubted that I would ever have the chance."

In 1937 *Life* published a feature article introducing the dude ranch to the world. This helped put the Murrays on solid financial ground. By the end of the 1930s, the property had twenty buildings and offered lodging, dining, horseback riding, and swimming. There was also a fenced-in baseball diamond and a tennis court. Two Black westerns, released in 1939, *Harlem Rides the Range* and *The Bronze Buckaroo*, were filmed there.

Over the next decade, Murray's gained in popularity with celebrities such as Lena Horne and Hedda Hopper, and it wasn't long before it made the cover of *Ebony* magazine. Boxer Joe Louis trained there in the 1940s, which caught the attention of *Life* magazine photographers who were in town to work on another story.

Paul Williams, a Black architect, also vacationed at Murray's. Williams was well known among Hollywood stars, having designed homes for Frank Sinatra, Zsa Zsa Gabor, Tyrone Power, and Anthony Quinn, as well as a few hundred residences in Beverly Hills and Bel Air. In the 1940s Williams designed elements of the Ambassador Hotel, a *Green Book* site that became infamous after Senator Robert F. Kennedy was assassinated there; and in the 1960s he collaborated with designers to build the futuristic structures at the Los Angeles Airport.

Former site of the Murray's Dude Ranch

Murray's was fully integrated, and was one of the first sites in this part of the country where white and Black children played and swam together. After seeing Black and white children together, a white woman staying at a nearby ranch wrote a story about how much it had touched her.

As Murray's became more popular, it received even more attention, praise, and inquiries from all over the country. Lela made sure to inform all the people interested in coming to the ranch that Black people owned it. And they came anyway. The Murrays hosted about one hundred people every week.

After Murray's, it was another seventy miles on Route 66 to Pasadena, California. This wasn't a good place to stop: There were no *Green Book* sites, and some of the pools in Pasadena allowed Black people to swim only on "International Day," which was usually on a Wednesday, the day before the pool was cleaned. Leaving Pasadena, Route 66 then dipped into the busy streets of downtown Los Angeles.

Downtown's most memorable *Green Book* site was Clifton's Cafeteria on Broadway, a sprawling five-story restaurant located right at the original terminus of Route 66. Diners entered through a wood-paneled tunnel that led to a wonderland of singing birds in a fake redwood forest with terraces, a fireplace, and shrubbery hanging from the walls.

Clifton's was originally owned by Clifford Clinton, a white man who was the son of Christian missionaries. As a boy, Clinton traveled with his parents to China, where he witnessed brutal and abject poverty firsthand. Back home, he couldn't understand how America, a country with so much wealth, could allow its citizens to go hungry. When he opened up his own restaurant, he never turned anyone away—even those who couldn't pay. Clinton followed what he called the "Cafeteria Golden Rule." His menu read, "Pay What You Wish" and "Dine Free Unless Delighted."

There were several Clifton's in Los Angeles. The Route 66 location opened just before the first *Green Book* was published but wasn't listed until 1957. (Another Clifton's, located downtown, was listed in earlier editions.) It may have helped that Clinton had several other restaurants in Los Angeles, but his altruism generated free publicity, which turned out to be good for business. At its height, Clifton's served fifteen thousand people a day, and celebrities ranging from Beat writer Jack Kerouac to entrepreneur Walt Disney to science fiction author Ray Bradbury were regulars.

Although the experience most Black motorists had on Route 66 couldn't have been more different from that of the average white American, it's comforting to know that they could count on Clifton's. It was the perfect place to end this epic journey.

Although Nat King Cole sang the Mother Road's catchy anthem, telling motorists to "get your kicks on Route 66," the carefree adventure he was promoting was not meant for him or other Black Americans. But despite the dangers, driving Route 66 was a risk that many Black motorists were willing to take, as the call of the open road seduced them just as it did other Americans. And it's not that Route 66 was more dangerous than other trans-American road trips. What makes Route 66 different is the branding associated with it. The "Mother Road" lives on in the hearts of tourists as a beacon of American travel. It became a global icon and is still the most celebrated highway of its time.

Front and interior of Clifton's Cafeteria, a former *Green Book* restaurant in Los Angeles, California, 2016

Route 66 was at the height of its popularity in 1957, a time when Black Americans were still fighting for their fundamental human rights. This was the year *Leave It to Beaver* premiered on CBS, Elvis Presley appeared from the waist up on *The Ed Sullivan Show,* and Jack Kerouac's novel *On the Road* was published. But this was also the year the Arkansas National Guard descended on Little Rock to stop nine Black students from entering Central High School and U.S. Senator Strom Thurmond staged a twenty-four-hour, eighteen-minute filibuster to block a civil rights bill being proposed in Congress. It was the longest filibuster that ever had taken place on the Senate floor.

In its heyday Route 66 was a complex network of roads that connected cities and towns through many different configurations and alignments. The most significant factor that changed it was the arrival of the Interstate Highway System. The photo of the freeway on-ramp on the cover of the 1957 *Green Book* was a sign of progress, signifying the arrival of an efficient way to travel throughout the country. Freeways offered a faster way to deliver goods, and the trucking industry supplied stable employment to Americans. Ironically, it was this same Interstate Highway System that killed Route 66. By the 1960s five interstates bypassed all the small Route 66 towns, and as a result, many fell into ruin.

The Interstate Highway System was mostly to blame, but Route 66 wasn't its only casualty. The freeway system was tied into "urban renewal" projects that spanned America, which not only took tourism away from Route 66 towns but also decimated Black communities. Urban renewal's effect on Black neighborhoods was even more destructive, as many of the new freeways bisected more Black communities than white.

In the name of "urban renewal," the U.S. government seized many *Green Book* sites under the statute of eminent domain, and Black-owned homes and businesses were bulldozed to make way for "progress." But this wasn't progress. Freeways created physical and psychological barriers, dividing a nation that was already struggling to find common ground. And although this was a time when the country thought it was moving forward, the pendulum was actually swinging backward—and this time, when it did, it literally became a wrecking ball.

Chapter 9

WOMEN AND THE GREEN BOOK

The *Green Book* played a critical role in the lives of women. Whether they were traveling across the country or running a hotel, beauty shop, or tourist home, women broke out of traditional gender roles. By the 1959 edition, a woman was in charge of the entire *Green Book* operation. Alma Duke Green was now listed as the editor and publisher of the guide, and nearly all her staff members were female. Victor Green acted as an adviser for this edition, but given that he would die in 1960, it's possible he was ill and unable to

Two women standing in front of a car, 1941

Victor H. Green

Alma D. Green

Edith Greene

Dorothy Asch

Evelyn Woolfolk

Novera Dashiell

Page of staff members listed in the *Green Book*, 1961

work. In any case, Alma was the perfect person to pick up the baton, because she had been right alongside her husband since he started the guide in 1936.

Assistant editor Novera Dashiell brought a different energy and tone to the *Green Book*. Dashiell's pieces were practical, her written voice was personable and direct, and her appearance reflected these attributes. She wore short, stylish Marcel waves in her hair, and her decisive eyebrows framed her no-nonsense glasses. Her articles were the few in the *Green Book*s with a byline.

With her frank, straightforward approach, Dashiell represented a refreshing new voice for the *Green Book*, and her content took a more political turn than Victor Green's had shown. For example, in one article, she refers to "tense world affairs," and writes, "Until the fear of war eases, we trust you will use your discretion in limiting your itinerary to the South American and East Indian areas."

With Dashiell's strong point of view, she appears to be right there with the reader. In the twentieth-anniversary edition, her pride is clearly on the page when she writes about the development and growth of the *Green Book*. It's almost as if she's talking about her own child. "After twenty years in circulation there are many things to wax sentimental about in retrospect. The conception, the first stumbling steps, difficulties in adolescence, then the ripening years of maturity; when at long last the realization of fulfilment."

Dashiell didn't mince words. She described her fellow staff member Dorothy Asch, the *Green Book*'s public relations representative, as the only "non-Negro member of the staff," and assures readers that even though Asch wasn't Black, "she works just as hard and her aims coincide with ours in the desire that the *Green Book* be the best available for the purpose it serves."

Asch and Dashiell were joined by Evelyn Woolfolk, the *Green Book*'s advertising correspondent. Woolfolk was possibly the longest-serving *Green Book* staff member. She started working for Victor Green in the 1930s, as a secretary, and continuing until 1942, when the *Green Book* had taken a break from publication due to World War II. During that hiatus, Woolfolk moved to Cleveland, Ohio, and resumed working for the *Green Book* in the 1950s.

When Woolfolk left in the 1940s, Edith Greene filled in as the secretary. She started working for Victor the year she graduated from business school and was described by Dashiell as their "girl Friday," entrusted with a wide variety of tasks.

Although women ran the 1959 edition, its format isn't very different from the previous edition, with the exception of a couple of pieces. A mail-in form was designed with a rating system so readers could share information about businesses they thought should be listed. Also, an article at the end of the edition, entitled "How to Guard Your Home During the Vacation Season," offered tips on how to "keep the thief away from your door." Most of the suggestions are what you would expect—setting lights on automatic timers, insuring valuables, discontinuing milk and newspaper delivery, alerting neighbors to your absence, and asking them to pick up your mail. The most interesting suggestion was to notify the police of your absence so they could check on your property. This reflects a time when the Black community not only knew their local police but also trusted them enough to ask for help.

Although Victor is often credited as the sole publisher and creator of the *Green Book*, Alma's role and influence shouldn't be overlooked. It's unknown exactly how much work she did, but it's likely she was a critical force behind the success and longevity of the guide. She also undoubtedly worked on the *Green Book* while Victor was a full-time postman for thirty-nine years.

Their marriage, it seems, was a true partnership. Victor and Alma had applied for their marriage license in Brooklyn, on September 8, 1917, nearly two decades before the first *Green Book* was published. Alma was about twenty-seven years old when she decided to marry Victor. An attractive and strong-looking woman, she was light-skinned—possibly of mixed race, she was listed as "mulatto" on the 1910 census and then as "Black" on the 1920 census—with short, curly hair, distinct features, and a solid frame. Alma lived another eighteen years after she lost Victor, dying in March 1978.

Between the ages of four and six, Alma's niece Sara Lawrence-Lightfoot would go to the Greens' house every day after school, along with her brother and sister. Sara remembered that the Greens kept a nicely appointed, comfortable, and fashionable home. And it was spotless. Sara's sister, Paula Wehmiller, writes about her memories of those days at the Greens' house in the 1950s:

After a long day at . . . an all-white private school on the Upper East Side of Manhattan . . . while our parents were still at work, we got dropped off uptown at Aunt Alma and Uncle Bob's [Alma's brother] house at 155th and St. Nicholas in Harlem.

Aunt Alma was married to handsome Uncle Victor who was a postman and wore a uniform. I loved to be at the kitchen table when Uncle Victor came in after his rounds. He'd put his postman's cap upside down on the table and hike his blue-gray trousers up as he straddled one of Aunt Alma's yellow vinyl chairs. His legs were so long that his knees met the edge of the table. Aunt Alma had already poured the coffee . . . He'd bring the cup expertly up to his lips and pull the liquid into his mouth with a delicious slurp. Uncle Victor and the coffee were the same color, and that was the part I liked the best.

Through the French doors off of the front room . . . [was Aunt Alma's dressing room]. This is where my sister and I spent the afternoons, playing in front of the mirror at Aunt Alma's dressing table. Pink and blue and purple crystally bottles with fancy diamond-shaped or spherical or pointy tops held sweet potions and perfumes for us to dab on our necks and wrists the way we saw Aunt Alma do. Some of the bottles had squeeze balls with fancy golden nets around them . . . It was here after a long day at a school full of people who looked unlike me, after a day of struggling with puzzling images, that I came home to myself.

A former *Green Book* tourist home in Pueblo, Colorado

At a time when they couldn't get credit from a bank or even have their own bank account, Black women found a measure of success and independence by listing their businesses in the *Green Book*. In the states where hotel options in the *Green Book* were limited, Black travelers often stayed in tourist homes. These became popular after the Depression and were run primarily by married women who rented rooms in their houses. Renting out rooms was a way for families of all races to earn extra income.

More than fourteen hundred tourist homes were listed in the *Green Book* during its publication. The tourist home was the great equalizer. Those who couldn't afford a hotel could likely afford a tourist home. Visiting a private home could leave a lasting impression. Unlike commercial spaces, they were personal and intimate. Every piece of furniture and art and each photograph, plant, curtain, and knickknack had been collected over years and handpicked by the owner.

Gary Kirksey's grandmother owned a *Green Book* tourist home, in Alliance, Ohio. He remembers: "It was a very large brown house. There was a parlor, restrooms upstairs and downstairs. There was a grape arbor in the back and a screened-in porch for people to relax all summer long."

Tourist homes were also the perfect place to build social networks because they were intimate, relaxing environments where vacationers could let their guard down, share a meal, tell a few stories, and make memories. In states where no *Green Book* hotels were listed, tourist homes could be lifesavers. In fact, 90 percent of all the *Green Book* sites in Nebraska and Michigan (except in Detroit) were tourist homes.

Tourist homes were also places where Black travelers were sure to get a warm meal. Usually, if they were in a town with no commercial *Green Book* restaurants, they had to fill up on cold cuts from grocery stores. Some cities, such as Springfield, Illinois, listed fourteen tourist homes, but during the entire time the *Green Book* was in publication, not one restaurant there was listed.

In addition to tourist homes, the *Green Book* featured traditionally "female" businesses, such as hair salons and beauty colleges. There were just under nine hundred beauty shops listed in the *Green Book* during its life. St. Louis, Missouri; Buffalo, New York; Kansas City, Missouri; and Wilmington, North Carolina, listed twice as many hair salons as they did food and lodging options. Other cities had an even wider disparity between salons and hotels. For example, Boston had forty-three salons and sixteen restaurants but only five hotels. San Antonio had fifteen beauty shops and five hotels, while Milwaukee had fifteen salons but only two hotels.

The uneven ratio of hotels to salons in the *Green Book* wasn't intentional on the editor's part. Most likely there were simply more Black-owned beauty shops than hotels—which was no surprise. Beauty salons were active, long-standing businesses in a community, providing a safe place where people could sit for hours. Amid the aroma of corrosive chemicals and the clicking of curling irons, customers could let down their hair, literally and figuratively, and spill their secrets in the comfort of cushioned vinyl.

Salon operators were not just hairstylists; they were pillars of the community. During the time salons were listed in the *Green Book*, some of them served as headquarters for community development, especially during the birth of the civil rights movement. At election time stylists drove their clients to the voting booth, and since the NAACP was considered a radical organization, some clients had its literature delivered to the beauty shop instead of to their homes. And you could usually find a copy of the *Chicago Defender* sitting on tables in the waiting area or in the magazine racks between hair dryers next to *Jet* and *Ebony*.

Of the seventeen beauty schools listed in the *Green Book*, the two most popular were Madam C. J. Walker's College of Beauty Culture and Annie M. Turnbo Malone's Poro Colleges. Malone started the Poro schools in 1917. They were scattered throughout the United States, including in New Orleans; St. Louis and Jefferson City, Missouri; and Cincinnati and Cleveland, Ohio. In addition to teaching cosmetology, Poro Colleges served as retail outlets, selling hair products for men as well as women. The Parkway Street location in Chicago was listed in the *Green Book*, and Earl Hutchinson remembers going to that one and said, "You could buy every type of hair dressing product."

Madam C. J. Walker's advertisement in the *Green Book*, 1960

Walker and Malone revolutionized the Black hair care industry by creating unique products to condition, grow, and straighten hair, which resulted in unprecedented wealth for both entrepreneurs. They trained thousands of women throughout the nation to use their hairstyling techniques, who then sold their products from door to door, and ran their own businesses. Working for Walker or Malone offered independence, power, and freedom from cleaning up after white people. As the automobile industry lifted Black men out of poverty and into the middle class, the hair industry did the same for Black women.

The Velvatex College of Beauty Culture in Little Rock, Arkansas, another *Green Book* site, is still in operation. In the early 1950s, its president, Mary Ellen Patterson, who established sorority chapters of the service organization Alpha Phi Omega throughout the state, took her students to do hair for free twice a month at the state hospital for the mentally ill. Updates on what was happening at the Velvatex College were regularly covered in the *Pittsburgh Courier*, and the *Chicago Defender* featured Velvatex news by celebrating the school's graduates.

In addition to beauty shops, another female-branded *Green Book* site was the Young Women's Christian Association (YWCA). Founded in 1855, the YWCA is one of the oldest women's organizations in the country and a pioneer in women's and civil rights. The first African American branch opened in Dayton, Ohio, in 1889. In the 1930s the YWCA encouraged its members to take a stand against lynching, and by the 1940s the organization had rallied to end racially segregated housing throughout the country.

YWCAs also provided much-needed lodging for women, and helped Black women find employment, guiding them on how to dress and prepare themselves for interviews. They were a welcome asset in the community.

The *Green Book* listed forty-seven YWCAs, and three of them were named after the legendary Phillis Wheatley, the first Black female poet published in America. Phillis arrived in Boston in 1761 on a slave ship and was purchased by John Wheatley. Wheatley's wife recognized that Phillis had a unique talent with words and supported her education. By 1773 she had been emancipated from slavery and had published a book of her poetry. Over the following century, Phillis Wheatley became a celebrated symbol of creativity and intelligence, as her poems inspired abolitionists and civil rights leaders. In addition to the YWCAs, eight *Green Book* hotels were named after her.

Phillis Wheatley Hotel, a former *Green Book* site in Cleveland, Ohio

Green Book YWCAs and lodging facilities named after women were critically important to female travelers, as they signaled a welcome to a segment of society often seen as second-class citizens. In the period the *Green Book* was in publication, traveling alone for women was still frowned upon. Not only were women restricted from renting rooms in reputable hotels, but some hotel policies wouldn't even allow them in the lobby if they were unaccompanied by a man. When traveling with a man, women were often advised by etiquette books to be discreet and stay out of public view. And in some cases it wasn't unusual for them to be directed to a "ladies' entrance."

It wasn't just at hotels that women were being scrutinized. Police and property owners were on high alert when a single woman appeared in a neighborhood. In fact, when police stopped waitresses walking home from work and found their tip money, they often accused them of being prostitutes. It was considered suspect for any woman to be carrying cash.

Another remarkable Black businesswoman was Ms. Geneva Haugabrooks, who ran a funeral home on Auburn Street in Atlanta. Her husband drowned soon after she opened in 1929, and she never remarried. She began the business with only three hundred dollars and kept it going until 1977. During its height, she buried about a thousand people a year. Marcus Wimby—Geneva was his grandfather's aunt—runs the business today. "Mama" Haugabrooks knew everybody in town, he told me. She would sit on the porch and wave at people who passed by and tell them, "I'm gonna get you one day. I'm gonna get you one day."

Mama Haugabrooks was an easygoing but also very powerful woman. "She owned Atlanta," Marcus said. "She went to the Cadillac dealership on Spring

Street . . . she wasn't well dressed or anything, so the salesman didn't think she had any money, so he blew her off. The manager knew who she was . . . fired the salesman, [saying], 'Do you know who you just disrespected? That's Ms. Geneva Haugabrooks.' Because she would buy three or four [Cadillacs] at a time."

Mama Haugabrooks even had clout with law enforcement. As Marcus remembers, after one of her employees was picked up by the police, when he said he worked for Ms. Haugabrooks, the white police officer didn't take him to jail. He took him to Ms. Haugabrooks and asked, "What do you want me to do with him?"

Scores of other women owned sites listed in the *Green Book*, but one woman, Mary Jane Elizabeth Colter, actually built one: the El Navajo, in Gallup, New Mexico.

Colter was an Irish woman with dark features, a robust nose, and full lips. Called an "incomprehensible woman in pants," she rode horseback "making sketches of prehistoric pueblo ruins, studying details of construction." These descriptions of Colter make sense because, in the early twentieth century, she was the head architect and interior designer for the Fred Harvey Company that had an exclusive contract with the National Park Service. While most Americans treasured European culture and design, Colter loved the look of the great Spanish and Mexican haciendas, feeling that the designs rooted in Native American, Spanish, and Mexican cultures were undervalued and ignored.

Colter pioneered an architectural style that blended Spanish Colonial and Mission Revival designs and used colors, textures, and surfaces native to the surrounding southwestern landscape. She was unique because she brought these outdoor elements inside, a radical idea for the time. Colter was also one of the first women to become prominent in the profession, and she revolutionized the field of interior design and architecture.

Colter is considered one of the most important architects of the early twentieth century. She was confident in her designs and rarely yielded to a man's will. When she designed a hotel at the bottom of the Grand Canyon, she decided to call it "Phantom Ranch," an allusion to the area's mystery and intrigue and referencing nearby Phantom Creek. The national park liked Colter's designs but not the name. During a meeting, she snatched the plans away, saying she wouldn't agree to the name change. "Not if you are going to be using my work," she said. She won the battle and built Phantom Ranch at the base of one of the largest canyons in the world. It opened in 1922 and was one of the signature works of her career. In 1918 Colter designed Gallup's Santa Fe railroad station, and in 1923, just west of the depot, she built the El Navajo Hotel and restaurant, which was listed in the 1957 *Green Book*. Unfortunately, to widen Route 66, the El Navajo was destroyed the same year it was listed in the *Green Book,* and Colter died a year later.

Just as Mary Colter triumphed in the male-dominated profession of architecture, another woman tied to the *Green Book* made her mark in another male-dominated industry—the world of politics. Her name was Modjeska Simkins.

Simkins set up NAACP chapters throughout the state of South Carolina, so she knew firsthand how difficult it was to get services while traveling. "I worked on the road eleven years," she remembers. "And no matter if I'd have $500 in my pocket, which I didn't have ... I couldn't buy a hot biscuit if I wanted one on the road. Especially small towns, there was no hot food available."

H-1892   EL NAVAJO, FRED HARVEY HOTEL, GALLUP, NEW MEXICO (AFTER PAINTING BY FRED GEARY)

The El Navajo, a *Green Book* hotel in Gallup, New Mexico

Along with Frank E. Bethel, Simkins co-owned Motel Simbeth, a *Green Book* site in Columbia, South Carolina. The motel offered a warm meal and cottages that could be rented by the day, week, or month. They were arranged in a semicircle nestled in a wooded area eight miles north of Columbia, on U.S. Highway 1. The Simbeth was advertised as having "Exclusive Accommodations for Colored Tourists . . . Among the whispering pines."

Simkins was born in 1899 and remembers, "My great-grandmother [and] my grandmother was a slave, and my father was born in [18]70, which is just five years after freedom." She wasn't sheltered from the harsh realities of racism. In fact, her mother read to her about the lynchings that were happening, and her family spoke frankly about the horrors of white supremacy.

So when white supremacists shot up her motel at 8:50 p.m. on March 15, 1956, Simkins wasn't rattled. It was the second time that week that Motel Simbeth's neon Colored sign had been smashed and littered with bullets. The first time, the perpetrators had not only shot up the other side of the sign, but also fired at the porch, near the office. The Simbeth staff were unable to identify the perpetrators in the dark, and the gunmen (or others) came back the following month and shot up the place again.

When reporters came out to cover the story, Simkins didn't have much to say about white terrorism. Later, in an interview about the Ku Klux Klan, she said, "I don't even hate the Ku Klux Klan, because if they're fool enough to do what they want to do . . . just so they don't come here and step off that sidewalk onto my walkway . . . they can build a cross right out there if they want to, but don't come up on my porch."

Simkins was fearless, outspoken, and knew her history. She was also a highly intelligent woman, teaching medieval history and civics at Benedict College. She fought to equalize teachers' salaries and get bus transportation for those who needed it, and she frequently spoke out against taxation without representation. She spearheaded a statewide campaign that eventually dismantled the white primary election so that Black people could vote. Columbia finally celebrated Simkins in 1991, when the mayor of the city declared December 5 as Modjeska Monteith Simkins Day.

Like all the women in this chapter who thrived in the midst of relentless sexism and racism, Simkins spoke to every woman who has been dismissed or told to step aside. After the Democratic Party tried to oust her from the party, she stood firm and said, "I wasn't moving. That was my answer."

Throughout the *Green Book* years, gutsy female business owners and single female travelers exuded an air of independence and navigated the country in a way that most men and society frowned upon—and yet they did it anyway.

Chapter 10

A CHANGE IS GONNA COME

The 1960s was one of the most defining decades of the twentieth century for Black Americans. Otis Redding released his hit "A Change Is Gonna Come," and the Black Power movement emerged, making Americans of all races examine and redefine what "Blackness" meant. Chemically processed hair was out, and the afro was in. As Black Americans were literally feeling their roots, their stance in the culture was anchored in a strong, upright posture. The quiet, passive, concealed approach was no

Green Book cover, 1960

longer the plan. It's as if the previous decades' attempts and failures at integration were the grit that pushed the oyster to make the pearl. By the end of the decade, James Brown told his brethren to "Say it loud. I'm Black and I'm proud!"

An afro appeared on the cover of the *Green Book* for the first time in the 1960 edition, making it one of the most political editions of the series. The afro is worn by a young Black figure. His head sits at the top left side of the cover, behind a large globe of the world. The size of the globe and the head are so similar, it gives the impression they are one and the same. His head is positioned higher than the globe, and it covers his left eye, but it's evident that the world is sitting right in front of him. He's omnipotent—looking at the world and beyond it at the same time. This cover is also striking because it's the first time we see a person who is unmistakably Black on it. Nearly all the figures on previous *Green Book* covers had fair skin with Anglo features that could have passed as white.

Another significant change in the 1960 edition is that the word *Negro* has been removed from the title. Instead of being *The Negro Travelers' Green Book*, it's simply *The Travelers' Green Book*. We don't miss the word *Negro* because once we see this definitive illustration of a Black figure on the cover, it's clear it is for Black people.

It isn't surprising that the *Green Book* was published for twenty-five years before a Black figure with traditional African features graced the cover. In American culture, beauty was (and often still is) defined as having light skin. This isn't to suggest that Victor Green found only light-skinned people attractive, but it does speak to the fact that he was living in a society that

The Black fist Afro pick, a symbol of the Black Power movement, signifies Black pride and identity. This pick belonged to Ron Burford.

revered lightness. The *Green Book* wasn't unique. This oppressive, narrow image of beauty was pervasive in Black newspapers and magazines. It was and still is a powerful form of oppression.

Although it is wrong and hurtful to shun those with rich, maple-toned skin, being lighter has its advantages—especially in America. In the 1950s, fair-skinned Black travelers might be allowed to stay in a motel with the requirement that, if asked, he or she would agree to say they were Mexican. Wellington Cox-Howard III, a light-skinned man from Mississippi, drove west with his father in the 1960s, without a *Green Book*, and was looking for a hotel. "We were in Kansas or Colorado, someplace where you wouldn't expect segregation," he remembers. "This was in the sixties. My father was [of a medium-brown] complexion, so he would send me in [saying], 'Go on in there and get the room . . . Put your cap on.' . . . I'd know how to get the room and give the money and everything and then they'd see my father and say, 'Hey, hold on! Who's that?'"

This aversion to darker skin is called "colorism." In America colorism was born in the antebellum South, when lighter-skinned Black slaves were chosen over darker-skinned slaves to be house servants. Colorism isn't unique to America; it's an attitude that's way too common all over the world. Although this stigma was planted by American slaveholders, over time it has been upheld by the Black community itself. The most blatant manifestation of this was the "brown paper bag test," a cruel, humiliating exercise in which a paper bag was held next to the face or arm of a Black person to see how his or her skin tone compared to the color of the bag. If the person was darker, he or she didn't "pass" and therefore wouldn't be admitted to the Black party, sorority, nightclub, or dance. Lighter skin opened doors into higher echelons of Black society. Even Black churches and Black universities used the paper bag test in their application process.

Since the Jim Crow era, colorism intensified and then waned, but in the twenty-first century, it's more complicated. In some cases it depends on where in the country one lives. Espresso-toned women such as actress Lupita Nyong'o are heralded as the pinnacle of beauty, and most major cities have embraced kinky hair. Chemical-free "natural salons" have opened throughout the country, and big, beautiful, tightly coiled curls can be seen regularly in the media.

Although it appears that more Black Americans love the skin and hair they were born with, the scars of white supremacy run deep, and in some pockets of the country, colorism still reigns. And overall, America is still a place where darker people are subjected to more violence and discrimination. When his wife, who is white, was expecting their first child, Stefan Wehmeyer, a Black man, said, "I prayed that she'd look white, and she does. She will be safe."

It's heartbreaking for Stefan to live in a country where he's afraid to see his skin color in his own child, but as long as Black people are twenty times more likely to get shot and Black women are twice as likely to be arrested than white women, it's understandable why he feels this way.

The fact that Wehmeyer lives in Sullivan, Missouri, a former sundown town on Route 66, may well have contributed to his feelings. In 2017, one year before he said that he hoped his daughter would look white, the NAACP issued its statewide travel advisory for Black people driving in Missouri.

Soon after, more Black Americans began thinking that the *Green Book* should be revived as a tool to keep them safe. Unfortunately, "driving while Black" is still a risky endeavor, and even though the *Green Book* could provide information about safe accommodations, Black travelers would still have to drive through dangerous locations to get to these places of sanctuary. A revived *Green Book* wouldn't ensure their safety on the highway.

The *Green Book*'s popularity continued to grow. By 1962, the *Pittsburgh Courier* reported that the *Green Book* had a circulation of two million. The 1960s was a time when there were more Black drivers on the road than there had ever been. Four out of five Black families owned cars, and three out of four cars were new. The *Chicago Defender* published an article stating that car ownership had risen to "record levels" and that Black families were spending "more than one billion dollars a year for auto travel." Black families were finally living a stable middle-class life, and an impressive car was the outward representation of that status. In the introduction to the 1961 *Green Book*, editor Novera Dashiell writes, "With greater job opportunities, higher incomes and paid vacations the Negro has come into his own." For many Black families, the pendulum of equality in the form of financial security was swinging forward, but unfortunately, money couldn't buy equal treatment. The *Defender* article also reported that although more Black people were purchasing cars, racism in the auto industry hadn't changed with the times. "There have been a bare minimum of Negro auto salesmen in showrooms for years, and little has been done in direct advertising . . . in Negro newspapers, or in other media to reach the Negro car buyer . . . There is still a timidity about actively selling to the Negro. There are few showrooms in

Negro communities, few Negro auto salesmen . . . There are some in the auto field, who predict that the first big company that aggressively goes out to sell to the Negro will reap a bonanza in sales. But the saying around Detroit and the auto ad agencies is that 'No one wants to get his feet wet first.'"

Chrysler became the exception to this, and broke the mold when, in November 1963, it offered Ed Davis, a Black man, his own dealership. After being in the business for twenty-eight years, Davis became the first Black man to own a dealership from one of the "Big Three" auto manufacturers.

Ed Davis featured in the *Detroit Free Press*

Davis was forty-nine years old when he signed with Chrysler. He had a fleet estimated at between seven hundred fifty and one thousand new automobiles, and he employed fifty-three people. Chrysler estimated that Davis would sell two hundred fifty automobiles his first year, but he doubled that figure. And within a few years, he was selling nearly a thousand cars, grossing about six million dollars annually. The *Detroit Free Press* reported that Davis "never relied on Chrysler for a single penny of financing."

Davis's dealership was on the Black side of town, but he was so good at what he did that within a few years, his white customer base rose from 3 percent to 20 percent. This crossover effect inspired other automobile companies to work with Black auto dealers. Change was finally happening in the industry, and just as in the late 1930s, the automobile again became a powerful symbol of progress. By the end of the 1960s, fourteen Black men had car dealerships. Of the 14, Ford trained six Black dealers, and Chrysler trained seven.

Significant change was happening for the *Green Book* as well. In 1961 Alma Green published the Silver Anniversary edition. Over its twenty-five-year tenure, the *Green Book* had grown from a ten-page pamphlet to a 128-page book. And although it was still sold at Esso stations, it could be purchased also on newsstands and in Gimbels department store in New York City. By the 1960s the *Green Book* had subscribers from all over the world, including Canada, Mexico, the West Indies, England, and West Africa. Achieving that level of distribution at a time when there was no Internet, and when long-distance calls were expensive, was astounding.

In Novera Dashiell's opening statement in the 1961 edition, she looks back over the *Green Book*'s twenty-five-year history. "We have come over a

Police dogs attack demonstrators, Birmingham protests, 1963

rocky terrain of obstacles and hurdles since 1936. Remember the years of the thirties and forties, when travel to and from any given point was an ordeal if you did not have a copy of the *Green Book*?"

Addressing race head-on, Dashiell writes candidly about racial freedom and the impact of the sit-in demonstrations happening all over the country. Change was happening both within the *Green Book* offices and out on the streets, and it was becoming increasingly clear that Black Americans were no longer going to silently accept second-class citizenship.

Although in the 1960s some cities, such as St. Louis, opened all their restaurants and cafés to Black patrons, and segregation in airports was substantially reduced, finding accommodation on the road was still a hit-or-miss proposition. Don Norman remembers driving up the California coast in 1962, while on his honeymoon. "It was late, so we stopped at the first motel we saw in Salinas. There was only one car in the parking lot . . . When we asked for a room, [he said] they were all full, but you could look at the back wall and see that practically every key was there . . . He never called us a curse word or a racially charged word, but we left. We were on Highway 1, it was pitch black and too dangerous to drive, so we stopped one more time[,] at another motel. I think this was called Seaside. We went in, and there was an elderly woman behind the counter. She said, 'Can I help you?' And I said, 'We're looking for a room, but I guess you won't give us one.' And she said, 'Why?' I said, 'Because we're Negro.' She said, 'That's silly. How many rooms do you need?' I said, 'One.' We explained to her that we had just gotten married. She gave us a key to the room. About twenty minutes later there was a knock on the door, and I thought, *Maybe she didn't realize we're Black.* We opened the door, and she had a tea service and a piece of homemade cake, and that made me feel like all is right with the world."

Being served at white-owned establishments was getting a little easier in the 1960s, but even these minor wins didn't happen without strategy and sacrifice. Black Americans were still fighting on the front lines, sitting on stools at lunch counters, and staging boycotts and protests that spilled onto the streets and into living rooms through television screens. As much as the *Green Book* excelled at presenting an ideal solution in the midst of a dangerous reality, by the 1960s the protests, riots, and bombings happening throughout America were too serious to ignore, and the *Green Book* stepped on board to aid in the civil rights struggle.

As Dashiell writes in her introduction, "Every age across recorded time, had its minority group pinioned in the talons of prejudice. Each race had its torch-bearers. History shows the rewards gained when a race made its own struggle against the ebb and flow of local and national passions. No one esteems freedom given or sought without it being earned. We have had our torch-bearers . . . 1960 has been quite an eventful year for Negroes in both domestic and foreign affairs. Our young generation with their successful sit-in demonstrations have prodded the older generation to greater effort in the struggle for civic dignity."

Dashiell was likely referring to the efforts led by Ella Baker, who organized the founding conference of the Student Nonviolent Coordinating Committee (SNCC), at Shaw University, in Raleigh, North Carolina, on April 17, 1960. SNCC was one of the most powerful and influential civil rights groups of the sixties.

Change came to the *Green Book* again in 1963, when Alma Green decided to have Langley P. Waller and Melvin Tapley copublish the 1963–64 and 1966–67 editions—the final two editions. Waller, who had a lithography shop, was the first Black printer for the *Amsterdam News,* a popular Harlem newspaper, and printed posters for the Apollo Theater and for boxer Sugar Ray Robinson. It's unknown how, or if, he knew Victor Green, but he clearly knew about the *Green Book,* because his lithography shop on Lenox Avenue was listed in the 1949 edition.

Melvin Tapley was the editorial cartoonist for the *New York Amsterdam News*. Tapley had illustrated the *Green Book* as well, creating the cover art for the 1959 edition and the image of the figure with the afro that appears on the

27th Consecutive Issue

FOUNDED 1936

By Victor H. Green

Travelers' GREEN BOOK
"Assured Protection for the Negro Traveler"

1963-64 EDITION
Published by
VICTOR H. GREEN CO.

L. A. WALLER
MELVIN TAPLEY
Co-Publishers

This edition of Travelers' Green Book is dedicated to our many friends and advertisers whose cooperation and encouragement made it possible: Mrs. Alma Green, Reginald Pierrepointe, Carlton Bertrand, Atty. J. J. Fieulleteau, Atty. Hope Stevens, Constance Curtis, Al Lockhart, William Capitman, Hy Schneider, Wendell Colton, Peter Celliers, Ken Brown, Thomasina Norford, Dr. P. M. H. Savory, Ted Shearer, Vondel Nichols, Frank Palumbo, and YOU.

LOCKHART AGENCY

Cover by
WILLARD SMITH

Possibly Langley Waller's daughter, *Green Book* contents page, 1963–1964

cover of the 1960 edition. Tapley was described as "quiet" and "soft-spoken," but he communicated a loud message in his politics. He was the president of the Peekskill, New York, NAACP chapter and won numerous awards for his art, including the top prize offered by the National Newspaper Publishers Association for excellence in editorial cartoons. He received his bachelor of arts degree from New York University and a certificate in art from Cooper Union, and he attended Columbia University for his master's degree. He continued drawing for the *New York Amsterdam News* into the 1990s.

The *Green Book* editions published under Waller and Tapley were double-year issues, the 1963–64 edition and the 1966–67 edition. (There appears not to have been a 1965 edition.) Although the *Green Book* was under new leadership, the masthead for the 1963–64 edition still lists "Victor H. Green and Co." as the publisher, and Alma Green is the first person to be thanked in the dedication section, as someone "whose cooperation and encouragement made it possible." Also on the masthead is a photograph of a smiling Black woman hugging a palm tree and holding a coconut shell drink in her hands. It is thought to be Waller's daughter.

Although the *Green Book* was given the tagline *International Guide* as far back as the 1949 edition, Waller and Tapley added *International* to the main title, and these last two editions were, in fact, more global than the others had been, with nearly seven pages of European accommodations and listings for sites throughout South America and in more than thirty countries in Africa.

It's clear the guide is in new hands when readers turn to page two and see in bold Black letters at the top of the page, "YOUR RIGHTS, BRIEFLY SPEAKING!" along with a photo of men the editors call "Rights

Guardians." These include congressmen from Illinois, California, New York, Pennsylvania, and Michigan. Also listed are organizations fighting for Black peoples' rights, such as CORE, the NAACP, and SNCC.

The article "Civil Rights: Facts vs. Fiction" opens up with a simple, yet powerful statement: "Most people who 'go on holiday,' as they say in England, the Caribbean and other places where the accent is English, are seeking someplace that offers them rest, relaxation and a refuge from the cares and worries of the work-a-day world. The Negro traveler, to whom the *Travelers' Green Book* has dedicated its efforts since 1936, is no exception. He, too, is looking for 'Vacation Without Aggravation.' . . . the Negro is only demanding what everyone else wants . . . what is guaranteed to all citizens by the Constitution of the United States."

Using words such as *demanding* signaled a new tone for the *Green Book*. The article outlines antidiscrimination laws for thirty states so travelers know their rights. It also gives readers information on what they could do if they are refused service or treated poorly. In addition, every U.S. Civil Rights Commission office is listed by state.

According to this article, Black travelers had no recourse for bad treatment in Montana, New Mexico, or West Virginia, because there were no anti–Jim Crow laws on the books in those states yet. But civil rights violators were subject to criminal punishment in Alaska; Colorado; Connecticut; Washington, DC; Illinois; Indiana; Iowa; Minnesota; Nebraska; New Jersey; New York; North Dakota; Ohio; Oregon; Pennsylvania; Vermont; Washington; Wisconsin; and Wyoming. Discriminatory advertising was off-limits in Colorado, Connecticut, Maine, Massachusetts, New Jersey, New York, and Washington State. Black people who were discriminated against could sue for damages in California, Idaho, Massachusetts, Michigan, Minnesota, New Jersey, New York, Ohio, Oregon, Pennsylvania, and Wisconsin. And violators could lose their business licenses in Michigan and Washington, DC. The place with the most punitive repercussions, however, wasn't on the mainland; if a business in the U.S. Virgin Islands discriminated against a Black person, violators could lose their license and be sued for damages up to five thousand dollars.

Also in these final two editions, Tapley illustrated a section called *Green Book*'s History Makers," a celebration of successful Black figures in history. One was Jim Beckwourth, a cowboy and fur trapper, and one of the founders of Denver. Another "History Maker" was a man named William Leidesdorff, who built San Francisco's first hotel and was reported to be the first Black millionaire in America.

"History Maker" Jim Beckwourth, *Green Book, 1963–1964*

The years spanning the publication of the final two *Green Books* were some of the most tumultuous in the country. Civil rights activist Medgar Evers was assassinated, and four precious little Black girls were killed in the bombing of the Sixteenth Street Baptist Church in Birmingham, Alabama. Los Angeles had one of its worst race riots, in Watts, and other riots broke out in Newark, New Jersey, and Detroit. It's prophetic that the 1963–64 edition ends with a large advertisement for Langston Hughes's book *Fight for Freedom*, which chronicles the fifty-four-year history of the NAACP. When this stage of the civil rights movement was under way, advertisements for books on racial freedom set the *Green Book* apart from other travel guides.

For unknown reasons, the *Green Book* took a hiatus in 1965. It's likely, though, that Waller and Tapley knew there would be a need for one last edition of the *Green Book*, which they put out in 1966.

In the 1966–67 edition, A. G. Gaston, a third *Green Book* "History Maker," was featured. A self-made millionaire and one of the most successful Black businessmen of

"History Maker" A. G. Gaston, *Green Book*, 1966-1967

the twentieth century, Gaston owned an insurance company, a chain of funeral homes, a savings and loan association, a farm, a business college, and a string of motels. He was a powerful man, and he used his money to challenge the status quo. When a white-owned bank hung a WHITES ONLY sign over its water fountain, Gaston threatened to withdraw his funds if it weren't removed.

Gaston's most significant hotel was the A. G. Gaston

A. G. Gaston (*right*) at his motel

Motel in Birmingham, Alabama, considered the best place for Black people to stay in the city. Before the Gaston, there hadn't been any dignified motels for Black people. Gaston had the place built in 1954, and two years later it was listed in the *Green Book*. A place where his community could feel safe to congregate, eat, and socialize, the Gaston featured thirty-two rooms with custom-made furnishings and was designed to serve high-class clientele.

Martin Luther King Jr. was the Gaston's most famous regular, holding meetings in what he called his "war room" to organize his troops. The Gaston became the headquarters for Dr. King's comprehensive integration campaigns, and it was here where it was decided that in order to support the local

Dr. Martin Luther King Jr. (*seated, left*) at the Gaston Motel, Birmingham, Alabama

protesters, King would go to jail. This was when he wrote his famous "Letter from Birmingham Jail."

King was at odds with Bull Connor, Birmingham's public safety commissioner. King thought things had been smoothed over, but two days after a truce was signed, just before midnight on May 11, 1963, the Gaston was bombed. There were no casualties, but four people were injured and most of the motel's façade was destroyed. King's younger brother's home was also bombed. These bombings didn't come without a warning. Earnest Gibson, the restaurant manager at the Gaston, had received a phone call the day before, telling him that the Ku Klux Klan was planning to bomb the motel. Officials at the Gaston informed the police in advance, but the attack still went off, without any interference from law enforcement.

After the bombing, about twenty-five-hundred people (mostly Black) rioted in the streets. They threw bricks, bottles, and rocks at police and firemen, slashed their tires, and set fire to six stores and a two-story apartment building. Fifty people were injured, and a policeman and taxi driver were stabbed.

King's executive director, Rev. Wyatt Tee Walker, emerged from the Gaston with a white handkerchief tied around his arm, calling for peace. Despite his urging the crowd to disperse and go home, the rioting continued until five in the morning. The *New York Times* reported that the police were out in full force, and the "thonk of clubs striking heads could be heard across the street."

Claude Sitton, the author of the *New York Times* piece, reported that King said, "Violence was the 'tactic of the white man' and he urged Negroes not to adopt it." The piece acknowledged that the night the Gaston was bombed, the message wasn't working. "Today's riots, like those that greeted the arrival of the Freedom Riders here two years ago[,] came on Mother's Day," Sitton wrote. "One difference was that in the previous outburst, whites were attacking Negroes."

It was clear that in the fight for civil rights, the tide had turned, and Black Americans were being pushed to their limit. A "change was gonna come" by any means necessary.

Travelers'
Green
Book

International
Edition 1966-67

FOR VACATION
WITHOUT
AGGRAVATION!

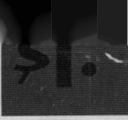

$1.⁰

HOTELS

MOTELS

CAMPS

VACATION RESORTS

EATERIES

TOURIST HOMES

Chapter 11

INTEGRATION

AND THE DOUBLE-EDGED SWORD OF

PROGRESS

Just from the cover, it's evident that the final *Green Book* edition of 1966–67 was unlike any other that had been published before. It has a lighthearted, kitschy spirit, and for the first time since 1940, the color green is gone, replaced by turquoise and magenta. An illustration of a woman is featured waterskiing and snow skiing simultaneously, wearing a snowsuit on one half of her body and a bikini on the other. This *Green Book* opens up to a full-page portrait of a man, most likely Langley Waller, one of

Green Book cover, 1966–1967

Langley Waller, publisher of the *Green Book*, 1966-1967

the new publishers, and for the first time in the guide's history, there is an entire section on U.S. parades, more than four pages on camps, and a listing of nineteen caverns to visit.

The final cover is joyful and fun, but inside, the more serious political tenor that had emerged in the 1960 edition continues. This last issue was the only one published after the passage of the 1964 Civil Rights Act, and it informs the reader immediately (on the second page) that there is "a new bill of rights for everyone, regardless of race, creed or color. Public Accommodations: Effective at once, every hotel, restaurant, theater or other facility catering to the general public must do exactly that."

The 1964 Civil Rights Act was the change Victor Green had dreamed about but did not live to see. His quote, appearing in the introduction for several editions, bears repeating again: "There will be a day sometime in the near future when this guide will not have to be published. That is when we as a race will have equal opportunities and privileges in the United States. It will be a great day for us to suspend this publication[,] for then we can go wherever we please, and without embarrassment."

President Lyndon Johnson shakes Martin Luther King Jr.'s hand at the signing of the 1964 Civil Rights Act.

The 1964 act was the sixth civil rights bill that had been passed since the abolishment of slavery. The first one was written in 1866, one year after passage of the Thirteenth Amendment that abolished slavery. Another was passed five years after that, to protect Black Americans from the relentless terrorism of the Ku Klux Klan. Four years later, in 1875, another law made it illegal to ban Black people from jury duty, public transportation, and public accommodations—but that didn't work, because by 1883 the U.S. Supreme Court had decided that portions of the act were unconstitutional. It wasn't until seventy-four years later that the next piece of civil rights legislation was passed. The Civil Rights Act of 1957 was supposed to protect voting rights as well. Clearly it wasn't effective because, eight years later (and one year after the 1964 Civil Rights Act was passed), three marches took place in Selma, Alabama, to demand fair and equal voting practices for Black people. During the first protest, on March 7, 1965, known as "Bloody Sunday," approximately six hundred marchers were doused with tear gas and beaten with bullwhips, billy clubs, and cattle prods outside the county courthouse in Selma. More than one hundred people were injured and more than fifty hospitalized. It seems that after all the failed attempts to legislate equality, most Black Americans were right not to expect the 1964 Civil Rights Act to be the salve that healed all wounds.

This is not to say the 1964 Civil Rights Act wasn't important. It was a critical step toward swinging the pendulum of equality forward, but it didn't happen without a great deal of pressure from the sit-ins and other protests led by popular African American organizations such as SNCC, CORE, the NAACP, and Martin Luther King Jr.'s cohorts and colleagues. Their concerted efforts pushed the federal government into passing this landmark legislation.

In the wake of the Civil Rights Act, white business owners found that desegregation increased profits by broadening their customer base, and it gave some of them the courage they had needed to do the right thing. Still, once the act passed, change didn't happen overnight. There were plenty of racist business owners who continued to refuse to serve Black Americans, in some cases finding devious loopholes to continue the legacy of segregation. In the South, some restaurants implemented a card-carrying system in which patrons now had to be "members" to receive service, and they made sure that no Black people ever joined their club.

But it wasn't just the South that used underhand tactics to keep Black patrons out. Other places served Black customers while finding ways to exploit them. Don Norman remembers going to Lawry's, a steakhouse in Los Angeles. "I was going to LA City College. I was working on the college newspaper. There was only one other Black person on staff [George]. He said, 'I'm never going to Lawry's again. They charged seven dollars and fifty cents for a prime rib dinner.' The editor of our paper said, 'No, that's not what they charge.' We both went [to Lawry's] and brought a date. Not knowing that there was a dual menu system, we noticed that the prices were higher. George and I almost simultaneously turned around to another table and asked to see a menu. It turned out that the prices at the other table, [whose occupants] happened to be white, were different. George asked to see the maître d' and he apologized profusely[,] saying that the prices had changed and we had the new menu. However, I noticed a gravy stain on the one I had. This turned out to be how we found out about the dual menu system."

Black patrons were rightfully frustrated with these scheming tactics of white-owned businesses, and many didn't want to spend their money at places that disrespected them. Paula Wynter remembers that, when she was a child, her father refused to patronize white-owned establishments. When they were on vacation, he told a Black hotel owner, "I'm not staying where they don't want me . . . I'm not going to eat in their establishments . . . I'm not going to patronize them in any way."

Once while traveling at night and using the *Green Book*, the Wynter family was driving on a two-lane blacktop highway in North Carolina. Paula remembers, "The sheriff is coming toward us in the opposite direction, and as we drive past, he makes a swift U-turn. My father had a new Buick [with] a New York license plate, and he was very conscious of the New York plates, and in these small towns they know everybody in the town . . . So, anyway, they made a quick U-turn, he [her father] gunned the motor to outrun them, because we were afraid if they stopped us they would kill him or harm us. We were in the car crying. My mother was hysterical . . . He drove really fast. He cut off his lights and took a side road really quickly and drove off down the road, and we sat under a tree until the sun came up. We saw the lights go past back and forth. They couldn't figure out where he was. It was really frightening. I was really young. [We stayed there until] daybreak. Afraid to go to sleep."

It's likely that the Civil Rights Act empowered Wynter's father. He could now choose where to spend his money. Black travelers were suddenly free to go anywhere and many wanted to try white businesses that had previously shut them out. So the new law ended up putting pressure on Black business owners to keep the customers they had. The editors of the *Green Book* were discerning enough to have addressed this issue three years before the passage of the Civil Rights Act. In the 1961 edition, editor Novera Dashiell writes, "He [the Black traveler] is selective. He is no longer content to pay top prices for inferior accommodations and services. White owners have come to realize the enormous economic power of the Negro. Conversely, our businessmen must now raise and maintain a higher standard to compete for our people's patronage."

Ultimately, the *Green Book* wanted Black tourists to have the same options that were available to white Americans. So, after desegregation, it listed white-owned luxury hotels that hadn't appeared in earlier editions, such as the Claremont, in Oakland, California; the Sir Francis Drake, in San Francisco; and the Benjamin Franklin, the place where Jackie Robinson had been denied service when he arrived in Philadelphia with his teammates in 1947. Waller and Tapley added even more high-end hotels, such as the Bel-Air, in Los Angeles; the Drake, in Chicago; and the Waldorf Astoria, in New York City. They also listed the top clothing stores, such as Brooks Brothers, Macy's, and Bergdorf Goodman.

The Drake Hotel, Chicago, Illinois, 2017

Including upscale establishments in the *Green Book* had its advantages, but the downside was that it took customers away from the Black-owned businesses that had been listed there for decades. In the 1956 edition, Victor Green had published a letter from the Nationwide Hotel Association (NHA), a Black hotel organization, warning Black businesses about this problem. The piece cautioned that in light of racial integration, the "Negro businessman is not prepared to enter the market serving all people. The NHA is aware of this problem and believes that the salvation of the Negro businessman, particularly in the hotel industry[,] lies in raising standards. Mr. Dykes Brookins said at a reception at the Dunbar Hotel in Washington, DC, 'I am convinced the Negro traveler would just as soon shop among his own if he could get—not comparable, but fair accommodations.'" A campaign to urge every NHA hotel owner to make improvements in his or her property in order to compete with white businesses was put in motion.

The problem wasn't just that some Black venues were "inferior." Once Black people could venture into new areas, they did. But as more Black travelers patronized white businesses, Black business owners lost the support they had relied on, and many struggled to keep their businesses open. It was a no-win situation. If Black travelers took their money elsewhere, it hurt their community. Yet, if they didn't go to these new places and show white Americans they deserved to be there just like anyone else, the country was never going to change. The stereotype that Black people couldn't afford to stay in nice hotels or were too animalistic or "wild" to assimilate into the upper crust of society had to be confronted.

Despite having access now, Black Americans were conflicted about pulling their money out of the Black community and spending it in white-owned establishments. Some Black business owners were even willing to take a financial hit for progress, such as the Black hotel owner who told Paula Wynter's father that it was important for him to go to white establishments.

"[Even though] I need your business . . ." he said. "I'm begging you. You have the money. Please go do it."

For the rest of their trip, the Wynter family stayed in white-owned hotels, but it wasn't a pleasant experience. Although the Civil Rights Act ensured that they could legally patronize public restaurants, there was no law to force someone to be kind to them when they arrived. Once, at a hotel near the border in Texas, they went into the dining room for dinner. Wynter remembers: "My mother had us in bows, you know, really dressed up, looking our absolute best. We step into the dining room. Silence. It was a really big room. Silence. Everybody stopped talking. Everybody turned and looked at us. It was terrifying. Not smiling. Scowling. Some people got up and walked out of the dining room as we walked in. We sat down. [My parents] ordered the food, and we ate. But it was not a fun memory. It was real scary to me, and very uncomfortable."

In less than a decade after the passage of the Civil Rights Act, at least half the *Green Book* Black-owned businesses were closed. One business that lost its battle with integration was the Dew Drop Inn, in New Orleans's Tremé district. Since Black tourists weren't welcome to stay in the French Quarter, most of New Orleans's *Green Book* sites had been located south of the quarter, along Rampart Street, in "Central City" and in Tremé.

The Dew Drop, on LaSalle Street, was a rare integrated nightclub. Frank G. Painia opened it in 1939. Although he only had a seventh-grade education, Painia knew how to run a business. He started by selling cold drinks to serve local laborers and then purchased a barbershop and a grocery store two doors down. The Dew Drop lived up to its original name, the

"Groove Room," when James Brown, Sam Cooke, Ike and Tina Turner, Otis Redding, and the fabulous Big Maybelle performed there. The nightclub was so popular that Little Richard wrote a song about it.

Female impersonators were also a staple at the Dew Drop. Sir Lady Java and Patsy Vidalia (born Irving Ale), a drag queen known as the "Toast of New Orleans," hosted the Dew Drop's annual Gay Ball. White gay men from the French Quarter made the nightclub a regular stop, mingling with Black and brown men, especially during the Gay Ball.

The Dew Drop, New Orleans, Louisiana, 1953

Inside the Dew Drop, New Orleans, Louisiana

The Dew Drop was beloved for its red beans and rice cooked in pig tails. Anywhere from two to three hundred people came each night, and the party could last until nine the next morning. Painia, always the businessman, tipped taxi drivers so they would bring tourists by. The place was so popular by 1945 that the *Louisiana Weekly* called it the swankiest nightclub in New Orleans.

The police regularly raided the Dew Drop because it served both Black and white people, which was illegal up until 1964. Painia grew tired of the raids, and after President Lyndon Johnson finally signed the Civil Rights Act, ending segregation in public accommodations, Painia sued the city of New Orleans in federal court, claiming that its race-mixing ordinance was unconstitutional.

The harassment stopped, but once Bourbon Street was open to Black patrons, they abandoned the Dew Drop to explore the French Quarter and its many restaurants, bars, and clubs. Ironically, it was integration, the very thing Painia had fought for, that killed the Dew Drop. It fell into decline during the end of the 1960s and closed for good in 1970.

A white mob attacking a Michigan car full of Black people passing through Tennessee in 1956

Unfortunately, integration was the reason most *Green Book* sites were lost. By the time the Dew Drop closed its doors, America had been struggling with integration since the landmark 1896 *Plessy v. Ferguson* decision, which was supposed to ensure that Black Americans had "separate but equal" public facilities, railway cars, and legal protection under the law. The promise of "separate but equal" was never delivered, and it took nearly sixty years of Black Americans receiving subhuman treatment before there was a legislative push for integration and *Brown v. Board of Education* overturned *Plessy v. Ferguson*. The first order of business was to integrate the schools. This was the most critical piece of legislation Black Americans of this generation had seen, and one of the key elements that ignited the civil rights movement.

Change rarely comes easily, but most Americans felt that, in theory, integration was the right thing to do. But in practice it was a significant hardship for both Black and white communities. As usual, the burden of this change weighed far heavier on Black Americans.

When desegregation began, protests and violence broke out all over the country, but even in situations where everything looked fine on the surface, being the first wave of Black students to attend an all-white school was traumatic for some children. Alma Green's niece Paula, who attended an all-white school on the Upper East Side of Manhattan, remembers, "For this little African American girl, it was a long day away from home, out to sea in an ocean of blonde strangers. It was a long day for a four-year-old to be in a world with no reflection of herself."

It took another decade after *Brown v. Board of Education* before any real progress was made. Some Black Americans didn't think that forced integration was worth all the problems. After living in a racist society, many had become experts at sheltering their children from the pain of segregation. Curtis Graves, an avid photographer, a Black legislator in the Texas House of Representatives, and director for civil affairs at NASA, used the *Green Book* to travel. "For the first six or seven years in my life, [my parents] lied a lot," he said. "For instance, we would go to one of the department stores downtown where there was a lunch counter, and I would say I wanted to have a Coke or I wanted to have a sandwich, and my mother would say, 'The glasses are not clean there.' And we would go home to have a Coke. She had a lie for everything that would have demoralized me. For instance, we didn't sit downstairs in the movie theater because 'it was cooler' upstairs. This was the story that I believed. The reason we sat at the back of the bus was that it was a better seat back there. In the front, 'it was too dusty and you wouldn't want to sit up in the front.' She had a story for every one of these indignities that I would have suffered as a child."

One year after the *Brown v. Board Education* decision, Mamie Till showed the world her son Emmett Till's disfigured body after he was beaten to death by white supremacists. Approximately three months after Till's murder, the Interstate Commerce Commission (ICC) banned racial segregation on interstate buses and in waiting areas. It considered the treatment of Black travelers "unreasonable" and cited the 1946 Supreme Court decision *Morgan v. Commonwealth of Virginia*, which found segregated bus travel unconstitutional. The ICC ban was a symbolic step forward, but in practice thirteen states still required segregated travel *within* their borders. It was not effective until 1961, when the Freedom Riders pressured Attorney General Robert F. Kennedy to enforce it.

Six days after the ICC ban, Rosa Parks was arrested for refusing to give up her seat to a white passenger on a city bus in Montgomery, Alabama. Parks said, "I thought of Emmett Till and when the bus driver ordered me to move to the back, I just couldn't move." Four days after Parks's arrest, the Montgomery Bus Boycott, led by Martin Luther King Jr., inspired Black residents to refuse to ride city buses for thirteen months. The boycott ended on December 20, 1956, when the U.S. Supreme Court finally ordered Montgomery, Alabama, to integrate its bus system.

Green Book sites were on the front lines in the battle for equality. From top to bottom, civil rights leaders were planning their next move. Before, during, and after the Montgomery Bus Boycott, Dr. King and his inner circle held secret meetings on the roof of the Ben Moore Hotel, a *Green Book* listing, while downstairs in the basement, Dr. King, Ralph Abernathy, officials from the NAACP, and other civil rights leaders socialized in the barbershop.

Since Black Montgomery residents weren't taking the bus downtown during the bus boycott, they did all their shopping in their own neighborhoods, supporting local, Black-owned businesses. And because they weren't spending their money on bus fare, even more money was being funneled back into the Black community. Supporting Black-owned businesses was critical to the success and the health of Black neighborhoods, not only in Montgomery but throughout the country as well. Black entrepreneurs rarely had access to capital, so it was hard enough to start a business, let alone maintain one, so they relied on a steady stream of Black patrons.

Many of the iconic Black-owned businesses, such as the Dew Drop Inn, fell on hard times after integration, becoming obscure, unrecognizable relics of the past. Another seminal New Orleans *Green Book* site that fell into obscurity was the Marsalis Mansion. It was located on the outskirts of New Orleans, and it offered lodging for Black tourists, who couldn't stay in the French Quarter.

The Hampton House in Miami was another important *Green Book* site that also lost its shine. When the owners, Harry and Florence Markowitz, a white Jewish couple, opened the Booker T. Washington Hotel (the original name of the Hampton House), they told the *Atlanta Daily World* that the hotel would "cater largely to high-class professional people, entertainers and other substantial Negroes visiting here." And it did. When world-renowned musicians such as Aretha Franklin, Sarah Vaughan, Count Basie, and Sammy Davis Jr. performed on Miami Beach, they couldn't stay in the Miami Beach hotels, so they traveled inland to the Brownsville neighborhood to stay at the Hampton House, where they'd often play a second, late-night set. It was during this second set, reserved for their peers, that the musicians let loose, relaxed, and performed the B-sides they didn't play for predominately white audiences. News of these jam sessions got out, and suddenly white folks were following these musicians to Hampton House, making it one of the most integrated hot spots in Miami.

Muhammad Ali stayed on the second floor, right above Dr. Martin Luther King Jr.'s room. (Ali first met Malcolm X at the Hampton House, and legend has it that it was this meeting that inspired the boxer to convert to Islam.) Civil rights organizations such as CORE met weekly in the hotel to implement desegregation policies, and Dr. King rehearsed his "I Have a Dream" speech there. Describing that day to filmmaker Kathy Hersh, civil rights activist A. D. Moore said, "It blew that place wide open. I'm telling you. He was fantastic."

Once Black people were allowed to frequent Miami Beach clubs, restaurants, and hotels, the Hampton House fell into decline. By the 1970s, the room where Dr. King stayed had become home to squatters, and a tree grew out of the pool he was once photographed in.

The Hampton House was on the verge of being demolished when, thankfully, Miami-Dade County invested millions of dollars in its restoration. Dr. Enid Pinkney spearheaded this effort, and since then, the Hampton House has undergone a full transformation. It reopened in May 2015.

Hampton House, a former *Green Book* hotel in Miami, Florida

It's ironic that it was integration, which most Americans wanted (and still want), that killed many of the sites in the *Green Book*. It's also ironic that something as hateful as segregation facilitated a stronger sense of unity in the Black community. Years of enforced isolation, seclusion, and fear of connecting with people outside one's race all came at a high price. All Black Americans wanted was the ability to walk, run, drive, shop, and live freely outside their neighborhoods, just like white people. After the Hampton House became another casualty to integration, community activist Georgia Ayers summed it up: "We got what we wanted, but we lost what we had."

Epilogue

AMERICA
AFTER THE
GREEN BOOK

I was riding in the front seat of our used baby-blue Volkswagen Bug with my mom. We were driving to the suburbs to visit family on the outskirts of Houston, Texas. It was 1978 and I was seven years old. As we approached the sugarcane fields, I saw figures dotting the landscape. As we got closer, I could see they were all Black men, and they were wearing chains. I turned and looked at Mom shocked, and said, "Isn't slavery over? They told us at school that slavery was over." She answered, "Yes, honey, it is." I looked

Convicts working in the American South , 1937

out the window and as we got closer, I saw Black men, bent at the waist, shackled, and sweating in Houston's oppressive heat and humidity. It looked so similar to the pictures I had seen in the history books of slaves working the fields. Shaking my head, I asked Mom again, "Why are they chained up?" She said, "They're prisoners." I looked at her, even more confused, and asked, "Well then why are they all Black?"

All I remember is silence. Perhaps she didn't know how to explain institutional racism to a seven-year-old, but I felt I was ready to have that conversation. I have been struggling with the image of that Black chain gang and questioning the existence of racial equality ever since. I couldn't believe what I was seeing, and the fact that my mother appeared to be so desensitized to it was mysterious to me. As I grew up, I began to understand why this wasn't shocking to her. She had watched this struggle for equality play out for decades, so when we drove past a Black chain gang in Texas, she took it in stride. But as a child, it was one of my most alarming and disturbing memories.

Nearly fifty years after that car ride, chain gangs are primarily a thing of the past. From the 1890s through the 1990s, prisoners would be chained together to work outside under the blazing sun with no protection, and usually the work was backbreaking. Even though today we don't see chain gangs on the side of the road, institutionalized racism is still alive and strong in the United States. It is a form of racism that has been normalized in our society, and as a result we have deeply engrained discrimination in nearly every American institution including the criminal justice system, employment, housing, education, politics, and health care.

Institutional racism in policing was discovered after a study was conducted in the town of Ferguson, Missouri. Route 66, the symbol of the American Dream, passed just a couple of miles north of Ferguson, the St. Louis suburb that made headlines in 2014 when Michael Brown laid dead in the street for four hours. Some who watched Brown bleed out onto the pavement called the event a modern-day lynching.

Ferguson was a sundown town until the mid-1960s, so perhaps the events that led up to Michael Brown's murder by a police officer are not surprising. Ferguson grew from a sundown town to having a Black population of nearly seventy percent today. One year after Brown was killed, the U.S. Department of Justice "found pervasive racial bias in Ferguson's policing and municipal court practices." The study also revealed that Black drivers in Ferguson were seventy-five percent more likely to be stopped and searched than whites. The statistics throughout the state of Missouri were consistent with what was happening in Ferguson. Now there was proof that Black motorists were being targeted, over-policed, and harassed, actions that presumably could not be limited to this one suburb. A year after the study was released things still weren't better in Missouri, so the NAACP issued a Black travel advisory for the entire state in 2017. The *Springfield News-Leader* ran the headline:

NAACP Warns Black Travelers To Use 'Extreme Caution' When Visiting Missouri

Acts of violence toward Black people have been the norm since the birth of the United States, and even before. From slavery to Jim Crow to today, the prejudice and divide between Black and white have been an American way of life. Some of these acts have been written off as random singular events, instigated by the "bad apples" in an otherwise just society. Today they bring to mind not only Michael Brown, but also many other names, including Trayvon Martin, Philando Castile, Tamir Rice, Alton B. Sterling, Sandra Bland, Freddie Gray, Walter Scott, and Eric Garner. More recently Breonna Taylor, Ahmaud Arbery, Tony McDade, and George Floyd can be added to that list. These violent encounters—instigated by both armed civilians and police officers that left mostly Black men and women dead—were widely publicized, so one can only imagine how many across the nation have gone unnoticed.

On August 12, 2017, a white supremacist group held the second day of a rally in Charlottesville, Virginia. They clashed with counterprotesters, leaving Heather Heyer, a white counterprotester, dead. Most of America was stunned by Heyer's murder and witnessing fresh-faced neo-Nazis in all-American khakis carrying lit tiki torches. It was too much. They insisted that this wasn't the America they knew. They were confused and devastated that the country they were so proud of was not living up to its promise of "freedom and justice for all." Many of my Black friends called me and said, "Well, here we go again" and "This is nothing new." But most of my white friends called me in tears. They were incensed by President Trump's racist rhetoric and terrified that we were losing the progress we made as a country since the election of our first Black president Barack Obama. I shared their anger, but I wondered why they weren't already outraged. Where had they been? For the last forty years, Black folks have been targeted, rounded up, and imprisoned under the watch of presidents Bill Clinton, the Bushes, and Barack Obama. No one seemed to care then.

While I was driving through Arkansas scouting *Green Book* sites, I took the Harrison exit off Highway 65. The town motto, "Adventure awaits you," unnerved me. I didn't see a sundown town sign, but there was an enormous white billboard on the highway with a large black *X* on a white background and the word *#secede* on it. I thought it looked familiar; then I realized the *X* was the same graphic that was printed on flags carried by the white supremacists in Charlottesville.

When neo-Nazis march through a city, people can no longer deny the role white supremacy is still playing in modern-day America. Millions were horrified at the brazen violence, and the crowd chanting "Jews will not replace us!" When President Trump refused to unequivocally denounce the neo-Nazis, America's image as a beacon of diversity and equality was spoiled for most Americans. They wanted to believe that the election of Barack Obama had finally solved our race problem. It had not. The events of Charlottesville swung the pendulum back to the nation's white supremacist roots.

Clearly, we still have work to do.

The loud, blatant prejudice toward Black Americans also has a silent partner. Robert J. Sampson, the author of *Great American City: Chicago and the Enduring Neighborhood Effect,* examined hypersegregated neighborhoods in Chicago from 2000 to 2005. While doing this research, Sampson found that Chicago's Black community had an imprisonment rate as a result of drug convictions over forty times higher than the surrounding white communities—even though white people use drugs at the same rates as Black people. Over a decade later, the Center for Spatial Research of Columbia University and the Justice Mapping Center used mapping software and discovered that Brooklyn, Chicago, and New Orleans spend more than one million dollars of taxpayer money, per city block, to incarcerate—imprison—its residents each year. They call them "million-dollar blocks." And they are generally located in traditional Black neighborhoods where *Green Book* sites had been clustered.

When asked why these Black neighborhoods are fraught with problems, the typical answer given by politicians is that there isn't enough money for education, housing, after-school programs, libraries, parks, and grocery stores. But this argument is clearly unreasonable because somehow the government can spend approximately eighty billion dollars locking up Americans for non-violent offenses and petty crimes such as unpaid traffic tickets, shoplifting, and minor parole violations. In some states it costs sixty thousand dollars a year to incarcerate one person. Imagine how that money could be redirected to support communities instead of tearing them down.

So when we look at American cities and wonder why there is so much violence, perhaps that is the wrong question. Given this history, why would we expect it to be any different? If you have two plants and give one everything it needs—sunshine, food, and water—and then you barely water the other one, you wouldn't expect the neglected plant to be as robust as the one that received nourishment, kindness, and attention. From this perspective, isn't it obvious that the unashamed and intentional neglect by the state and federal government bears significant responsibility for the state of inner-city neighborhoods—primarily Black—throughout America?

In 1967, the year the *Green Book* ceased publication, Martin Luther King Jr. spoke out against the Vietnam war, launched a war on poverty, and in June published his last book, *Where Do We Go From Here*? In the book King tells his readers that the fight for freedom is not over and that Black people will have to keep fighting for equal education, housing, voting rights, and jobs. A month later he delivered a sermon with the same title at the annual Southern Christian Leadership Conference in Atlanta, saying, "This is no time for romantic illusions and empty philosophical debates about freedom. This is a time for action. What is needed is a strategy for change, a tactical program that will bring the Negro into the mainstream of American life as quickly as possible. So far, this has only been offered by the nonviolent movement. Without recognizing this we will end up with solutions that don't solve, answers that don't answer, and explanations that don't explain . . . I'm concerned about justice."

One year after King delivered this speech he was killed at the Lorraine Motel, a *Green Book* site in Memphis, Tennessee. His assassination was a symbolic bullet to the change and progress the country had made with the passage of the 1964 Civil Rights Act. The pendulum of justice became a rudderless arm, and for a moment—everything stopped.

The same year we lost King, President Richard Nixon ramped up his predecessor Lyndon B. Johnson's "War on Crime" initiative into a "War on Drugs." He targeted Black neighborhoods where most *Green Book* businesses were located. President Nixon told his chief of staff, H. R. Haldeman, "You have to face the fact that the whole problem is really the blacks. The key is to devise a system that recognizes this while not appearing to . . . there has never in history been an adequate black nation—and they are the only race of which this is true. Africa is hopeless."

The Lorraine Motel, a former *Green Book* site and the place where Dr. Martin Luther King Jr. was assassinated (commemorated with a wreath). Today it is the home of the National Civil Rights Museum.

In many respects Nixon's "War on Drugs," which was a government-led initiative to stop the illegal sale and distribution of drugs, was supposed to be enforced throughout America, but it essentially became a war on Black communities. These were places where *Green Book* sites once thrived and apparently Nixon's plan worked. In over just one decade, after the *Green*

Book ceased publication, the number of Americans incarcerated had doubled. And today it has skyrocketed to seven hundred percent of what it was in the 1960s. The Justice Department now predicts that one in three Black male babies born in America will be incarcerated in their lifetime.

It isn't just Nixon who is responsible for the mass incarceration catastrophe we have today. Former president Bill Clinton's 1994 crime bill kicked the pendulum of justice further back than any failed policies that attempted to address racial equality since the Civil Rights Act was passed. In fact, nearly every U.S. president since Nixon has designed their own "get tough on crime" initiatives, but Clinton's crime bill was the worst. He signed three laws that brought irreparable damage to Black communities. His welfare reform act made it a crime for someone with a drug conviction to get food stamps or to live in public housing. His antiterrorist and death penalty act made it difficult to challenge wrongful convictions. As a result, there are many people sitting in prison today who don't belong there. And his prison reform act made it difficult for inmates to file charges, even when they were assaulted by a correctional officer, so the level of abuse and violence inflicted on prisoners has risen. As a result of this crime bill, those that survive prison leave deeply scarred and traumatized.

In addition to the 1994 crime bill, stop-and-frisk practices were implemented throughout the country, which also led to mass incarceration. Before stop-and-frisk was widely practiced, the Fourth Amendment required police officers to have probable cause, or a reasonable suspicion that a crime was being committed in order to pull someone over or stop them on the street. Stop-and-frisk loosened this law and allowed police to stop anyone at any time for any reason. Before, police had to get a warrant from a judge to search a citizen's property or their bodies; stop-and-frisk eliminated that. By 2013 a federal judge ruled that stop-and-frisk was unconstitutional, but by then the damage had already been done. These aggressive policing tactics were not used in white communities across the country. They were primarily used on Black people in disadvantaged neighborhoods. For instance, in places such as New York City, 83 percent of all the illegal stops conducted by police were on Black and brown people. Suddenly, there weren't enough prisons to hold everyone. Only two years after the crime bill was signed, seventeen billion dollars that had been allocated for public housing was being used to build prisons instead.

Once America had locked up nearly a third of its young Black men—many of whom had committed crimes that white people would not have gone to jail for—America had dug itself an even deeper hole. In Michelle Alexander's seminal book, *The New Jim Crow: Mass Incarceration in the Age of Color Blindness,* she states that more African Americans are under correctional control today than were enslaved in 1850, and the majority of felons have lost their right to vote, further marginalizing the Black community. In most states a felony record prevents convicts from receiving public housing, food stamps, student loans, or stable employment—essentially denying their ability to live a life as a free and equal citizen. For those who live in the underprivileged neighborhoods, all these government policies that targeted the Black community—redlining, urban renewal, the crime bill, and stop-and-frisk—guaranteed the incarceration of Black people and branded them felons for the rest of their lives. Since in many states the crime bill revoked a felon's right to vote, Alexander remarked that if President Barack Obama had been born on the South Side of Chicago, it's likely that he would have fallen victim to the system of mass incarceration, taking away his right to vote, let alone, become president of the United States.

My stepfather, Ron Burford, worked in the criminal justice system for forty years. He served as an assistant regional administrator, a parole counselor for the Ohio Youth Commission in Dayton, Ohio, and he was a probation officer for the U. S. District Courts in Cincinnati. While he worked in a southern Ohio police department, Ron was resented by other officers (all white). He believed he was treated badly because he was one of the only men there to have a master's degree. But Ron kept his head down and moved up the ranks until there were only five positions above him in the entire Ohio prison system.

Inside Alcatraz Federal Penitentiary, a former maximum security prison that sits off the coast of San Francisco, California. Today, it houses a museum.

After years of watching Black men go in and out of prison, Ron developed anti-recidivism programs that included everything from military boot camps to smoking cessation programs to yoga. The intent was to keep former prisoners from falling back to crime when they were released from prison. The problem was, no matter what he did, once they got into the system nothing seemed to free them of it. After Ron retired he mentored high school boys.

He wanted to help children who were buried in trauma and chained to circumstances that most would never overcome. His aim was to keep these boys out of prison and on the path to be a part of the community. So he coached football in a Columbus, Ohio, school that had some of the poorest students in the city. Rudasil was one of the young men he took under his wing, and he became part of our family. Ron was like a father to him. He helped him get into college, and within a year of Ron's passing, Rudasil earned a master's degree in business administration.

Ron Burford, 1960s

The issue of racism and mass incarceration is so close to my heart, because I see how many people (both white and Black) dismiss what I believe is the civil rights crisis of our time.

Why has our society over the years so freely accepted slavery, Jim Crow segregation, housing segregation, educational segregation, and now mass incarceration? Why are we willing to accept poverty, substandard schools, and subhuman treatment of Black people? And when I say "we," I mean Americans of every race. Diane McWhorter, the author of *A Dream of Freedom: The Civil Rights Movement from 1954 to 1968*, said in an interview about the widespread acceptance of racial segregation in the South, "You have to deform your conscience to accept something that is clearly wrong."

I believe this is what we are doing as a nation to accept mass incarceration. We must be clear and vigilant in our understanding of the past, question America's aspirational exceptionalism, and be honest about where this country has triumphed, and where it has failed. Until America reckons with its moral debt it will not live up to its own ideals.

If we want to live up to our values—one of our greatest challenges will be to dismantle and rebuild the criminal justice system. Ida B. Wells said, "The way to right wrongs is to turn the light of truth on them." But once we know the truth we have to take action. We now live in a country that has more prisons than universities. To help people leaving prison, Michelle Alexander, the author of *The New Jim Crow*, says we have got to end the shame and stigma that follows convicts for the rest of their lives. We need to build an "underground railroad" for them and help them to find jobs and housing.

The Eldorado, a former *Green Book* nightclub in Houston, Texas

When I started working on this project in 2013, most of the people I encountered had never heard of the *Green Book*. Many said, "Oh, thank God we don't need that anymore." Four years later, as more news reports showed unarmed Black people losing their lives at the hands of law enforcement, most Americans could no longer pretend that things were okay. While I was writing this book, every month another story would surface. Black people were being arrested and harassed for waiting at Starbucks, entering their Airbnb rentals, and swimming in a public pool. By 2018, when I mentioned the *Green Book*, the response changed from "Thank God those days are over" to "We need a modern-day version of the *Green Book*."

It's understandable why people think we need something to address the brazen display of white nationalist rhetoric—its propaganda and slogans—but since Black people are legally able to walk into any public establishment, a new *Green Book* will not make things better, because in many cases Black people are still feared in these public establishments. The *Green Book* provided listings of accommodations for Black-owned businesses and, yes, a guide that showcased today's Black-owned shops would be a great asset, but it couldn't guarantee that you could get to these places safely, or not be harassed by law enforcement, shot on the street, or discriminated against at the airport.

The *Green Book* was a formidable weapon in the fight for equal rights. It gave Black Americans permission to venture out on America's highways and enjoy the country they helped build. Victor Green probably didn't set out to create a weapon for change, but it's also likely that when Steve Jobs put a video camera in a phone, he didn't plan to trigger a new civil rights movement either, as it enabled people to record events on the street and have it used as proof of injustices. The point is, real change can come from simple tools that solve a problem. That is why the *Green Book* was so powerful.

More than a new *Green Book*, we need to learn from our past mistakes. This country was built on racism and if we're not careful, racism is the weapon that will destroy it. The pendulum will simply keep swinging back and forth until it breaks. There will be times when the fight for justice feels futile and pointless, but these are the battles worth fighting for. And if in another twenty, fifty, or one hundred years, we find ourselves scratching our heads wondering why America still isn't living up to its promise of freedom and equality for all, at some point we have to accept that we are all responsible. Just as the author and educator Jelani Cobb tells his students at Columbia University, "History doesn't repeat itself. Humans do."

Mom reading to
me in the 1970s

ACKNOWLEDGMENTS

This book is dedicated to my late mother, Carol Burford. She taught me to read and write before I even went to kindergarten. She fought for me throughout every stage of my life and without her steadfast love and guidance, I don't think I would have become an author. In the third grade, when my teacher in Houston held me back from the A-level reading/writing course because I was Black, (there were no Black children in the A-level courses), she fought for me. She pulled me out of the school and we moved to Ohio. The following month I tested out of third and fourth grade and started fifth grade. Over the course of my life, Mom supported my decision to be an artist and a writer and always encouraged me to keep going, especially when I didn't know how I was going to pay my bills. She was also my comrade on the road. For my first book, *Counter Culture*, she accompanied me on several trips to interview aging diner waitresses. She set up my photography equipment and put the waitresses at ease, ensuring that I could get the best interviews. And then at night we would stay in nice hotels and knit together. She was my best friend, and I miss her terribly.

This book would also have not been possible without my stepfather, Ron Burford; my sister Aimee Schwab; and my dear friends Sophie Pegrum, Valerie Boyd, and Robert Townsend. I am deeply grateful to my uncle, the brilliant photographer Adger Cowans. His encouragement, love, light, and wisdom gave me the emotional stamina and spiritual guidance I needed to write this book.

Overground Railroad would not be in your hands without the dogged determination of my incredible agent Chris Tomasino. She spent countless hours on the phone and crisscrossed the country, and the Atlantic Ocean, to tell everyone she could about this project. Chris is fierce, fearless, and always on my side, negotiating deals any author could dream of. Thanks also to her husband, Greg Bestick, who not only supports my work but who shared Chris with me on weekends, holidays, and during family celebrations so we could hash out our plans to get this out into the world. And once the contracts started coming in, I have to give a special thanks to Marea Parker, my intellectual property lawyer for protecting my vision and retaining as many rights as I could so I can continue to create future *Green Book*–related projects. The three of us combined are a force of nature.

The book would not have been possible without the financial support from the National Endowment for the Humanities (Public Scholar Award), the Library of Congress (Archie Green Fellowship), the American Council of Learned Societies (ACLS), the California Humanities, the Graham Foundation, the National Park Service, and National Geographic.

A special thank-you to Henry Louis Gates Jr. for honoring me with a Hutchins Fellowship Award at Harvard University. Being a Hutchins Fellow has been one of the highlights of my life. At Harvard, I formed inspiring and deep connections with some of the most brilliant minds I have ever encountered. Thank you, Ben and Krishna Lewis, Abby Wolf, and Dr. William Julius Wilson for supporting me while I was at Harvard and for believing in this project. And I offer deep gratitude and love to Dr. Cornel West for being a mentor and for getting on an early flight to make it to my presentation at Harvard.

My Scholar-in-Residence Fellowship at the Schomburg Center for Research in Black Culture gave me the tools and the resources I needed to produce a multilayered transmedia project with depth and substance. Thank you, Khalil Gibran Muhammad, Makiba Foster, Ayofemi Kirby, and Maira Lirano, the Schomburg's chief librarian, who provided valuable assistance with research. I'm also thankful to Brent Edwards for his brilliant insight and mentorship; my dear sister Aisha al-Adawiya for her soul-soothing hugs—and special thanks to Kevin Young for his guidance and support.

Thank you to Sarah K. Khan, who organized our beloved Ladies of the Committee, a group of brilliant and powerful women of color doing incredible work: Marie Brown, Sonya Y. Clark, Sylvia Lewis, Michele Washington, Deborah Willis, and Paulette Young. I cherish our brunches in Harlem. And thank you to the following artists, filmmakers, writers, administrators, educators, and media producers for their encouragement, love, support, and advice: Fredie Adelman, Krista and Doug Alexander, Harry Allen, Patrick Arbore, Kaisa Barthuli, Mark Bartlett, Stephen Beal, Tammy Belcher, Fran Benson, Adam Berg, Vanessa Broussard, Andrea Clardy, Patricia Clark, Stephanie Yawa De Wolfe, Michelle Delaney, Monica Duke, John T. Edge, Lolis Eric Elie, Thomas Fjallstam, Terri Freeman, David A. M. Goldberg, Jewelle Gomez, Nancy Groce, Vicki Hughes, Sandy Huntzinger, Diana Ingram, Peyton Jackson, John Jennings, Beth and Rich Lasky, Brent Leggs, Kathy Levitt, Michael Luongo, Deborah Martin, Lydia Matthews, Mike Miller, Diana Baird N'Diaye, Katrina Parks, Allene Payne, Michael Richter, Peter Samuels, Amy Scholder, Charice

Acknowledgments

Silverman, John Smith, Gloria Steinem, Sterling Storm, Kim Stringfellow, K.C. Thompson, Hank Willis Thomas, Mabel Wilson, and Julie Winokur.

Thank you to the Reservation Bureaus throughout the United States who helped secure lodging for me, and a special thanks to the following hotel chains that hosted me and offered free upgrades: Ace Hotel, Algonquin Hotel, Hilton, Hyatt, Marriott, the Pierre in New York City, and 21C Museum. You gave me something to look forward to at the end of those long days on the road.

Thank you to my team at the Smithsonian Institution Traveling Exhibition Service (SITES): Marquette Folley, Josette Cole, Haili Francis, Arlene Irizarry, Bob Leopold, Michelle Torres-Carmona, Austin Matthews, and Myriam Springuel.

Thank you to my *Green Book* "spouse," Calvin Ramsey, and his producer, Becky Wible Searles, for sharing their research and to all the *Green Book* business owners and associates who shared their time and their stories with me, including Leah Chase, Kenneth Christman Sr. and Patricia Christman Bailey, Ed Davis, Ollie Gates, Kenneth Jackson, Don Loper, Nelson Malden, Jerry Markowitz, Dr. Enid Pinkney, Herbert Sulaiman, David Swett, Dino Thompson, Rev. Alan Threatt, David Threatt, and the rest of the Threatt Family, Henrie Treadwell, and Marcus Wimby.

I am indebted to my research assistants Meley Araya, Claire Kim, and Craig Stevens.

And thank you to my editor at Abrams, Howard Reeves, and for the editorial support from Sophie Pegrum, Jill Petty, Chris Tomasino, Gary Tufel, and Julie Wolf.

NOTES

INTRODUCTION

ARE WE THERE YET?

xiv "Just What You Have Been Looking For!!": Victor H. Green, *The Negro Motorists' Green Book*. Leonia, NJ: Victor H. Green and Co., 1948, 61. (Hereafter, *Green Book* editions cited by year.)

xvi "There will be a day sometime in the near future": 1948 *Green Book*, 1.

xix Urban renewal. dsl.richmond.edu/panorama/ renewal/#view=0/0/1&viz=cartogram.

CHAPTER 1

THE BUSINESS OF THE *GREEN BOOK*

2 "Glener remembered seeing Victor Green": Howard Glener, in *The Green Book Chronicles*, from interview files producers shared with author.

2 "He had a manner about him": Ibid.

2 "The first edition was small": To my knowledge, no one has seen a copy of this edition. While I was a fellow at the Schomburg Center for Research in Black Culture we were unable to locate a copy of the first edition. This information is referenced from an article, "Travel Guide '61 Issue Set," *Chicago Defender*, May 20, 1961, p. 5, col. 4.

3 "There were at least six other Black travel guides": In the 1920s, there was another travel guide with "Green Book" in the title, *The ALA Automobile Green Book*, but it was not designed for Black travelers and had nothing to do with Victor Green's guide.

5   "He opened the 1939 edition": 1939 *Green Book*, 1.

5   "If not, tell us also, as we appreciate": 1948, 1949, 1950, and 1951
*Green Book*s.

5   "an excellent opportunity": 1940 *Green Book*, 24.

5   "Negro motoring conditions, scenic wonders": 1937, 1939, 1940, and 1941 *Green Book*s.

6   "It is a great pleasure for me": 1938, 1939, and 1940 *Green Book*s.

7   "Some reports have estimated that": Victor H. Green, "'Green Book' in
26th Year," *Pittsburgh Courier*, June 1962, 19.

7   "Green encouraged businesses": 1937 *Green Book*, 12.

CHAPTER 2

DRIVING WHILE BLACK

8   "Seven years had passed since the Great Depression": John George Van Deusen,
The Black Man in White America. Washington, DC: Associated Publishers Inc.,
1938, 69.

11   "There were no blacks on 125th Street": Ted Fox, "The Apollo Theater Before
125th Street Was the Black Main Street," *Huffington Post*, April 22, 2014.
See www.huffingtonpost.com/ted-fox/the-apollo-theater-before-125th-street
_b_4826811.html.

11   "He told a New York newspaper in 1937": Ibid.

12   "Welles hired local Haitians to perform": Stefan Andrews, "The Lafayette
Theater in Harlem became the first major theater which did not segregate
African-American audiences in New York," *Vintage News*, Feb. 20, 2017. See
www.thevintagenews.com/2017/02/20/the-lafayette-theater-in-harlem-became
-the-first-major-theater-which-did-not-segregate-african-american-audiences-in
-new-york.

14   "Then a brick flew through": "False rumors of a black Puerto Rican boy's death
sparks the Harlem riot of 1935," *New York Daily News*, March 18, 2015.
See www.nydailynews.com/new-york/nyc-crime/rumors-Black-boy-death-sparks
-harlem-riot-1935-article-1.2145887.

14   "But it wasn't only Blacks who were violent": Ibid.

14   "It concluded that the riot": Ibid.

15   "If we once make a religion of our determination": Maggie Anderson, *Our Black Year: One Family's Quest to Buy Black in America's Racially Divided Economy.* New York: Public Affairs/Hachette, 2012, 75.

17   "In New York City alone": 1938 *Green Book*, 11.

18   "Did you ever see a 'Jim-Crow' waiting-room?": W. E. B. Du Bois, *Darkwater: Voices from Within the Veil.* Project Gutenberg eBook, 2005. See www.gutenberg.org/files/15210/15210.txt.

19   "For instance, in the early 1930s": Warren Brown, "Cadillac's Cultural Turn." *Washington Post*, Dec. 24, 1995.

20   "By the mid-1930s": J. M. Packard, *American Nightmare: The History of Jim Crow.* New York: St. Martin's Griffin, 2003, 167.

21   "You had to be prepared": Herbert Sulaiman, interview with author. Myrtle Beach, SC: Dec. 8, 2018.

24   "On the road was a small Black community": Email correspondence with the author, July 21, 2017.

25   "As a Black man, he was forbidden": Doug Tatum, "Joe Bartholomew: The Times-Picayune Covers 175 Years of New Orleans History," *Times-Picayune*, Jan. 29, 2012.

26   "We should be doing no service": "The Tribune Speaks," *Chicago Defender*, Aug. 10, 1929, A2.

CHAPTER 3
THE FIGHT

34   "What kind of people do the officials": "Army Bans Segregation in Germany but Enforces It in United States," *Philadelphia Tribune*, Sept. 30, 1944, 4.

36   "in 1917, when the United States": Chad Williams, *Torchbearers of Democracy: African American Soldiers in the World War I Era.* Chapel Hill: University of North Carolina Press, 2010, 32.

37   "He was sitting in the back": Ambassador Theodore Britton, in *The Green Book Chronicles.*

39 "The need for full subscription": Spring 1947 *Green Book*, 3.

39 "The educated Negro": Ibid.

40 "For example, only two Black men": Brentin Mock, "How Discrimination Against Black Veterans Helped Shape Urban America," Bloomberg CityLab, Nov. 11, 2016. See citylab.com/equity/2016/11/how-discrimination-against-black -veterans-helped-shape-urban-america/507512.

41 "Black GIs being denied access": Tracy Jan, "White Families Have Nearly 10 Times the Net Worth of Black Families. And the Gap Is Growing," *Washington Post*, Sept. 28, 2017. See www.washingtonpost.com/news/wonk/wp/2017/09/28 /black-and-hispanic-families-are-making-more-money-but-they-still-lag-far -behind-whites/?utm_term=.02b4e97dfa22.

42 "I started to bite him, but he looked dirty": Richard Goldstein, "Irene Morgan Kirkaldy, 90, Rights Pioneer Dies," *New York Times*, Aug. 13, 2007.

43 "The hotel manager told the team's traveling secretary": Yanan Wang, "Philadelphia Apologizes to Jackie Robinson for the 'Unconscionable Abuse' He Once Suffered There," *Washington Post*, April 1, 2016.

CHAPTER 4

A LICENSE TO LEAVE

44 "They were state-sanctioned events": For more information about this history, read Sherrilyn A. Ifill's book *On the Courthouse Lawn*. Boston: Beacon Press, 2007.

46 "In some places, they put advertisements": Earl Ofari Hutchinson Sr., with Earl Ofari Hutchinson. *A Colored Man's Journey Through 20th Century Segregated America*. Los Angeles: Middle Passage Press, 2000, 14.

47 "If there was a lynching": Ibid., 35.

47 "An article written in the *Defender*": Jay Jackson, *Chicago Defender*, Jan. 4, 1936, p.1, col.1.

47 "A well-dressed Black family": Ibid.

50 "Earlean Lindsey, who migrated north": Earlean Lindsey, quoted in *The History of African American Women During the Great Migration*. YouTube. See www.youtube.com/watch?v=Eb43kOmEJ1k.

51   "From Chicago to St. Louis": Ramona Green, in *The Green Book Chronicles*.

51   "As Hutchinson wrote": Hutchinson Sr., with Hutchinson, *A Colored Man's Journey Through 20th Century Segregated America*, 87.

51   "Although roughly 1 percent": Van Deusen, *The Black Man in White America*, 70.

53   "In most cases, the clerk": Hutchinson, 87.

54   "When talking about Negroes": 1948 *Green Book*, 4.

54   "If one community reports": Langston Hughes, "The See-Saw of Race." *Chicago Defender*, April 20, 1946.

55   "Many Negroes still lived in overcrowded": Hutchinson, 30.

60   "Victor Green proudly called": 1949 *Green Book*, 23.

60   "It was a racket": Hutchinson, 31 and 33.

60   "People think this is a lie": Earlean Lindsey, quoted in *The History of African American Women During the Great Migration*.

60   "Well, in the South you": Curtis Coleman, quoted in *The History of African American Women During the Great Migration*.

61   "A typical statement": James W. Loewen, *Sundown Towns*. New York: New Press, 2005, 258.

CHAPTER 5
ALL ABOARD

70   "Five Points had more Black-owned businesses": "Known as the 'Harlem of the West,' Five Points, Denver, CO, was a predominately African American neighborhood." Smithsonian NMAAHC (@NMAAHC), Twitter, Nov. 3, 2018, 11:32 am. See twitter.com/NMAAHC /status/1058789063434493952.

73   "It begins with a glowing statement": 1951 *Green Book*, 13.

75   "Since white merchants ran": Paul Weeks, "Great Negro Tide Surges into Melting Pot of West," in *California: Promise and Problems. Los Angeles Times*, Sept. 17, 1962 3-4, Calisphere. See calisphere.org/item/ark:/13030 /hb8b69p5v8.

75   "Back then, Hutchinson wrote": Hutchinson Sr., with Hutchinson, *A Colored Man's Journey Through 20th Century Segregated America*, 90-91.

77 "Tom Bradley, Los Angeles's first Black mayor": "Historic Black Hotel Gets New Lease on Life." *Los Angeles Herald-Examiner*, April 24, 1987.

77 "Former president of the LA branch": "Kiwanis Club Will Honor Celes King." *Los Angeles Sentinel*, Sept. 15–21, 1994, A4.

CHAPTER 6

VACATION

82 "Victor Green said he changed": 1952 *Green Book*, 1.

86 "The two-page article describes Bermuda": 1949 *Green Book*, 76.

86 "They were featured in Black newspapers": Tiffany M. Gill, *Beauty Shop Politics*. Chicago: University of Illinois Press, 2010.

88 "A major difference between the treatment": Langston Hughes, "Major Differences Between Europe and America for Negro Theatrical Performers," *Chicago Defender*, May 23, 1953, 10.

91 "Shirley Coleman, the Hendersons' daughter": Shirley Coleman, in *The Green Book Chronicles*.

91 "It was a 'Dark Continent'": Ibid.

96 "And it went out about two hundred yards": Dino Thompson, in *The Green Book Chronicles*.

97 "And that's the way it was": Herbert Sulaiman, interview with author.

97 "The *Chicago Tribune* called it": Ken Armstrong, "The 1919 Race Riots," *Chicago Tribune*, Dec. 19, 2007. See www.chicagotribune.com/news/nationworld /politics/chi-chicagodays-raceriots-story-story.html.

100 "It was decided that": Kathleen Franz, "The Open Road: Automobility and Racial Uplift in the Interwar Years," in Bruce Sinclair, *Technology and the African American Experience*. Cambridge, MA: MIT Press, 2004, 137.

101 "As a result, only white men": Susan Shumaker, "Untold Stories from America's National Parks: Segregation in the National Parks." See www.pbs.org /nationalparks/media/pdfs/tnp-abi-untold-stories-pt-01-segregation.pdf.

102 "A survey of national park visitors": Rob Lovitt, *Where Are the People of Color in National Parks?* Aug. 3, 2011. See www.nbcnews.com/id/44008927/ns /travel-news/t/where-are-people-color-national-parks/#.XJ9a7utKjOQ.

102 "Why would I want to go?": Mireya Navarro, "National Parks Reach Out to Blacks Who Aren't Visiting," *New York Times*, Nov. 2, 2010. See www.nytimes.com/2010/11/03/science/earth/03parks.html.

CHAPTER 7

MUSIC VENUES

115 "It was like a little Vegas": Elizabeth Pepin, "Music of the Fillmore." Thirteen, PBS.org. See www.pbs.org/kqed/fillmore/learning/music/swing.html.

116 "The greatest Black music on earth": Dino Thompson, in *The Green Book Chronicles*.

116 "But you could go to Charlie's Place": Ibid.

116 "Stone told Wexler": Ibid.

117 "I just said, 'Well'": Ibid.

118 "Charlie said nonchalantly, 'Never noticed it'. . .": Ibid.

119 "A short, heavy Klansman": Interview with Charles Fitzgerald, Department of Justice. Washington, DC, Oct. 5, 1950, from files shared with author.

120 "The FBI report noted": Ibid.

120 "And they never spoke about it again": Dino Thompson, in *The Green Book Chronicles*.

121 "Dino Thompson summed it up": Ibid.

CHAPTER 8

THE ROOTS OF ROUTE 66

127 "When Earl Hutchinson left Chicago": Hutchinson, *A Colored Man's Journey*, 89.

127 "You knew that you couldn't eat": Ibid., 87.

129 "You could get . . . a sandwich": Robert Gaston interview, McLean County Museum of History, Bloomington, IL, Sept. 30, 2018.

130 "And I'm not sure if we will": Joe Sonderman interview, Missouri State University Libraries, May 18, 2015.

130 "When he sat next to a white classmate": Ed Pilkington, "From the Green Book to Facebook," Feb. 11, 2018. See www.theguardian.com/world/2018/feb/11/green -book-facebook-black-motorists-racist-america-road-trip-pitstops-safe.

135 "In less than twenty-four hours": The John Hope Franklin Center for Reconciliation offers space for healing, with a twenty-five-foot memorial and three sixteen-foot granite sculptures honoring the dead.

136 "I stopped with my entire": Preston Lauterbach, *The Chitlin' Circuit and the Road to Rock 'n' Roll.* New York and London: W. W. Norton, 2011, 51.

139 "They could not have found": "Motels Along Highway 66 Ban Negroes, NAACP Aide Says," *Albuquerque Tribune*, Aug. 16, 1955. See newspaperarchive.com/ politics-clipping-aug-16-1955-824703.

142 "I am a bachelor": Richard D. Thompson, *Murray's Ranch: Apple Valley's African- American Dude Ranch*, 5. See mojavehistory.com/murray5.html.

CHAPTER 9
WOMEN AND THE *GREEN BOOK*

151 "Until the fear of war eases": Novera Dashiell, "Having a Wonderful Time," 1957 Green Book, 55

151 "After twenty years in circulation": Novera Dashiell, "Many Happy Returns," Fall 1956 *Green Book*, 5.

151 "She described her fellow staff member": Novera Dashiell, "Janus," 1961 *Green Book*, 5.

152 "Also, an article at the end of the edition": Alma Green, "How to Guard Your Home During the Vacation Season," 1959 *Green Book*, 85.

153 "Alma was about twenty-seven years old": Alma Green's exact age is unknown. According to Social Security records, Alma was born in Virginia on June 9, 1889, but according to the 1910 Census, she was born in 1891.

153 "After a long day at . . . an all-white": Paula Lawrence-Wehmiller, "Face to Face: Lessons Learned on the Teaching Journey." Friends Council on Education, shared with the author.

155 "It was a very large brown house": Gary Kirksey, quoted in *The Green Book Chronicles*.

157   "The Parkway Street location": Hutchinson, *A Colored Man's Journey*, 38.

160   "I'm gonna get you one day": Marcus Wimby, interview with author, Atlanta, GA, Dec. 13, 2018.

161   "Called an 'incomprehensible woman in pants'": Richard Flint and Shirley Cushing Flint, "Mary Elizabeth Jane Colter." New Mexico History. See newmexicohistory
.org/people/mary-elizabeth-jane-colter.

161   "These descriptions of Colter": A recent book came out disputing her career as an architect, but until the information is verified, this is the legacy Colter has lived with for nearly a century.

162   "Not if you are going to be using my work": "Phantom Ranch." Grand Canyon National Park Lodges. See www.grandcanyonlodges.com/lodging
/phantom-ranch.

162   "I worked on the road eleven years": Isaac Washington, interview with Modjeska Simkins. WIS-TV *Awareness Story 12*, 1980, Moving Image Research Collections, University of South Carolina, Columbia.

163   "Simkins was born in 1899 and remembers": Jhan Robbins, Oral History Interview with Modjeska Simkins, Oct. 28, 1985. Walker Local and Family History Center, Richland Library, Columbia, SC.

164   "Later, in an interview about the Ku Klux Klan": Isaac Washington interview with Modjeska Simkins.

164   "That was my answer.": Ibid.

CHAPTER 10

A CHANGE IS GONNA COME

170   "We were in Kansas or Colorado": Wellington Cox-Howard, in *The Green Book Chronicles*.

171   "When his wife, who is white, was expecting their first": Pilkington, "From the Green Book to Facebook."

171   "It's heartbreaking for Stefan to live in a country": "Criminal Justice Fact Sheet," NAACP, 2015. See www.naacp.org/criminal-justice-fact-sheet.

Notes

172 "By 1962, the *Pittsburgh Courier* reported": "Green Book in Its 26th Year," *New Pittsburgh Courier*, June 1962, 19.

172 "The *Chicago Defender* published an article": "4 Out of 5 Negro Families in Cities Now Own Cars," *Chicago Defender*, Sept. 29, 1962, 4.

172 "In the introduction to the 1961 *Green Book*": Novera Dashiell, "Janus," 1961 *Green Book*, 4.

172 "There have been a bare minimum": "4 Out of 5 Negro Families in Cities Now Own Cars." *Chicago Defender*, Sept. 29, 1962, 4.

173 "But the saying around Detroit and the auto ad": Ibid.

174 "The *Detroit Free Press* reported that Davis": David C. Smith, "GM to Sign 2 Negro Dealers," *Detroit Free Press*, Sept. 3, 1967, 12A.

174 "Ford trained six Black dealers, and Chrysler trained seven": "14 Blacks Now Have Car Dealerships in Nation." *Chicago Defender*, May 31, 1969, 27, col. 1.

175 "Remember the years of the thirties and forties": Novera Dashiell, "Janus," 1961 *Green Book*, 4.

176 "It was late, so we stopped at the first": Don Norman, interview, "Southern Reconciliations," *StoryCorps*, April 28, 2018.

177 "Our young generation with their successful": Novera Dashiell, "Janus," 1961 *Green Book*, 4.

180 "Most people who 'go on holiday,'": "Your Rights, Briefly Speaking," 1963–64 *Green Book*, 2.

185 "The *New York Times* reported that the police": Claude Sitton, "50 Hurt in Negro Rioting After Birmingham Blasts," *New York Times*, May 13, 1963. See archive. nytimes.com/www.nytimes.com/library/national/race/051363race-ra.html.

185 "Claude Sitton, the author of the *New York Times* piece": Ibid.

185 "One difference was that in the previous outburst . . .": Ibid.

CHAPTER 11

INTEGRATION AND THE DOUBLE-EDGED SWORD OF PROGRESS

188 "It will be a great day for us to suspend": 1949 *Green Book*, 1.

191 "I was going to LA City College": Don Norman, interview, "Southern Reconciliations."

191 "The sheriff is coming": Paula Wynter, in *The Green Book Chronicles*.

192 "Conversely, our businessmen must now": Novera Dashiell, "Janus," 1961 Green Book, 4.

194 "Mr. Dykes Brookins said at a reception": 1956 Green Book, 69.

195 "[Even though] I need your business": Paula Wynter, in *The Green Book Chronicles*.

195 "My mother had us in bows, you know,": Ibid.

201 "For the first six or seven years in my life": Curtis Graves, quoted in *The Green Book Chronicles*.

203 "Describing that day to filmmaker Kathy Hersh": Roshan Nebhrajani, "The Hallowed Halls of the Hampton House Are Coming Back to Life," *New Tropic*, June 16, 2016.

205 "After the Hampton House became": Douglas Hanks, "For Hampton House, a Return from History." *Miami Herald*, Housing Finance Authority video. See www.miamiherald.com/news/local/community/miami-dade /article20557536.html.

EPILOGUE

AMERICA AFTER THE *GREEN BOOK*

209 "One year after Brown": "Ferguson police shooting suspect appears in court and enters no plea," *Guardian*, March 16, 2015.

Notes

212 "But this argument is clearly unreasonable": Criminal Justice Fact Sheet, NAACP, 2019. See www.naacp.org/criminal-justice-fact-sheet.

213 "Without recognizing this": Martin Luther King Jr., *The Radical King*. Boston: Beacon Press, 2015. See www.beacon.org/The-Radical-King-P1049.aspx.

213 "The key is to devise a system that recognizes": "Haldeman Diary Shows Nixon Was Wary of Blacks and Jews," *New York Times*, May 18, 1994. See www.nytimes.com/1994/05/18/us/haldeman-diary-shows-nixon-was-wary-of-blacks-and-jews.html. Also in John Ehrlichman, *Witness to Power: The Nixon Years* (New York: Simon & Schuster, 1982).

215 "The Justice Department now predicts": Patrick A. Langan, PhD, "Race of Prisoners Admitted to State and Federal Institutions, 1926–86." U.S. Department of Justice, May 1991. See www.ncjrs.gov/pdffiles1/nij/125618.pdf.

219 "Diane McWhorter . . . said in an interview. . .":: *Selma Q&A with Diane McWhorter*. University of Arizona School of Journalism–Tucson, filmed Feb. 6, 2016; posted May 24, 2016. See www.youtube.com/watch?v=g60hUJGH9p8.

SELECT BIBLIOGRAPHY

Adero, Malaika, ed. *Up South: Stories, Studies, and Letters of This Century's Black Migrations.* New York: The New Press, 1993.

Albuquerque Tribune. "Motels Along Highway 66 Ban Negroes, NAACP Aide Says." (Aug. 16, 1955).

Allen, James, et. al. *Without Sanctuary: Lynching Photography in America.* Santa Fe, NM: Twin Palms Publisher, 2000.

Amick, Marcus. "Ed Davis Is a Trailblazer in Auto Industry." *Michigan Chronicle* (Dec. 1998): C2.

Anbinder, Jacob. *Jim Crow Terminals: The Desegregation of American Airports.* Athens: University of Georgia Press, 2016.

Armstead, Myra B. Young. "Revisiting Hotels and Other Lodgings: American Tourist Spaces Through the Lens of Black Pleasure Travelers, 1880–1950." *Journal of Decorative and Propaganda Arts* 25 (2005): 136–59.

Atlanta Daily World. "Grayson' Travel Guide Off the Press." (1937): 4.

Barton, Craig Evan, ed. *Sites of Memory: Perspectives on Architecture and Race.* New York: Princeton Architectural Press, 2001.

Bay, Mia, and Ann Fabian. *Race and Retail: Consumption Across the Color Line.* New Brunswick, NJ: Rutgers University Press, 2015.

Belasco, James. *Americans on the Road: From Autocamp to Motel, 1910–1945.* Baltimore, MD: Johns Hopkins University Press, 1997.

Bliss, Laura. "Mapping Chicago's 'Million Dollar Blocks': The Costs of Incarceration Are Concentrated in Low-income, Predominantly Black Communities in the City." CityLab, July 24, 2015.

Boehm, Lisa Krissoff. *Making a Way Out of No Way.* Jackson: University Press of Mississippi, 2009.

Select Bibliography

Bowles, Gladys Kleinwort. *Net Migration of the Population, 1950–60: By Age, Sex, and Color*. Washington, DC: Economic Research Service, U.S. Dept. of Agriculture, 1965.

Bromwich, Johan Engel. "Airbnb Cancels Accounts Linked to White Nationalist Rally in Charlottesville." *New York Times* (Aug. 9, 2017).

Brown, Warren. "Cadillac's Cultural Turn." *Washington Post* (Dec. 24, 1995).

Bunche, Ralph J. "A Critique of New Deal Social Planning as It Affects Negroes." *Journal of Negro Education* 5, no. 1 (Jan. 1936): 59–65.

Caro, Robert A. *The Power Broker: Robert Moses and the Fall of New York*. New York: Alfred A. Knopf, 1974.

Chicago Defender. "Army Leaves Pershing Hotel." (Oct. 21, 1944): 3.

——. "Force Standard Oil to Drop Café Jim Crow." (Feb. 28, 1948): 1.

——. "4 Out of 5 Negro Families in Cities Now Own Cars." (Sept. 29, 1962): 4.

——. "14 Blacks Now Have Car Dealerships in Nation." (May 31, 1969): 27, col. 1.

——. "Judge Helps Defender Break Color Barrier." (April 15, 1939): 7.

——. "Link Lindy Flight to U.S. Lynchings." (Jan. 4, 1936): 1.

——. "Lynch-Bill Plea." (April 6, 1940): 6.

——. "Race Travel Is Helped by Tourist Aid." (June 18, 1938).

Clinton, Clifford. Boxes 1 and 10. Clifford Clinton Papers. UCLA Special Collections, Los Angeles, CA.

Coates, Ta-Nehisi. "The Case for Reparations." *Atlantic* (June 24, 2014).

Cuddy, G. A. *Where Hash Rules: The Love Story of Charlie's Sandwich Shoppe in Boston*. 2nd ed. Boston: CreateSpace Publishing, 2015.

Davis, Ed. *One Man's Way*. Detroit, MI: Edward Davis Associates, 1979.

Davis, George A., and Fred O. Donaldson. *Blacks in the United States: A Geographic Perspective*. Boston: Houghton Mifflin Co., 1975.

DeGraaf, Lawrence, Kevin Mulroy, and Quintard Taylor, eds. *Seeking El Dorado: African Americans in California*. Seattle: University of Washington Press, 2001.

Delmont, Matthew. "Why African-American Soldiers Saw World War II as a Two-Front Battle." *Smithsonian Magazine* (Aug. 24, 2017).

Dennis, Hevesi. "Activist Led One of the First Lunch Counter Sit-ins." *Globe and Mail* (June 15, 2011): S8.

Diggs, Rep. Charles C. Jr. to the President of Continental Airlines, March 12, 1955. See airandspace.si.edu/exhibitions/America-by-air/online/abalmage.cfm?webID=308.p7.

Dixon, Robert G., Jr., "Civil Rights in Air Transportation and Government Initiative."
    Virginia Law Review 49, no. 2 (March 1963): 205-31.

Du Bois, W. E. B. (William Edward Burghardt), 1868-1963. Dalton, Georgia, ca. March
    1932. W. E. B. Du Bois Papers (MS 312). Special Collections and University
    Archives, University of Massachusetts Amherst Libraries.

——. *Darkwater: Voices From Within the Veil.* New York: Dover, 1999.

——. "Race Relations in the United States." *Phylon,* 9, no. 3 (3rd Qtr., 1948): 234-47.

Ebony. "Why Negroes Buy Cadillacs." *Ebony* 4, no. 11 (1949): 34-35.

Equal Justic Initiative. *Lynching in America: Confronting the Legacy of Racial Terror.*
    2nd ed. Montgomery, AL: Equal Justice Initiative, 2015.

Feldman, Brian S. "Where Have All the Black-Owned Businesses Gone." CityLab,
    May 1, 2017.

Foote, Kenneth E. "Editing Memory and Automobility & Race: Two Learning Activities
    on Contested Heritage and Place." *Southeastern Geographer* 52, no. 4 (2012):
    384-97.

Ford, Larry, and Ernest Griffin. "The Ghettoization of Paradise." *Geographical Review*
    69 (1979).

Foster, Mark S. "In the Face of 'Jim Crow': Prosperous Blacks and Vacations, Travel
    and Outdoor Leisure, 1890-1945." *Journal of Negro History* 84, no. 2 (Spring
    1999): 130-49.

Franz, Kathleen, and Susan Smulyan. "African Americans Take to the Open Road." *Major
    Problems in American Popular Culture.* 1st ed. Boston: Cengage Learning, 2011: 240.

Frazier, E. Franklin. *Black Bourgeoisie: The Rise of a New Middle Class in the United
    States.* New York: Collier Books, 1962.

Froelich, Jacqueline, and David Zimmermann. "Total Eclipse: The Destruction of
    the African American Community of Harrison, Arkansas, in 1905 and 1909."
    Arkansas Historical Quarterly 58, no. 2 (Summer 1999): 131-59.

Gilroy, Paul. "Driving While Black." In Daniel Miller, ed., *Car Cultures.* Oxford, UK:
    Berg, 2001.

Glasrud, Bruce A. *African American History in New Mexico.* Albuquerque: University
    of New Mexico Press, 2013.

Goodwin, E. Marvin. *Black Migration in America from 1915 to 1960: An Uneasy Exodus.*
    Lewiston, NY: E. Mellon Press, 1990.

Select Bibliography

Grand Canyon News. "Arizona: Open Roads and Opportunities for African Americans." (Feb. 14, 2017).

Haman, Sidney. "Around the USA: Get Out Before Sundown!" *Nation* (Nov. 10, 1951): 2.

Harrison, Alferdteen, ed. *Black Exodus: The Great Migration from the American South.* Jackson: University Press of Mississippi, 1991.

Harrison, Sarah D. *The Travelers Guide.* Philadelphia, PA: Hackley and Harrison Publishing Company, 1931.

Holland, Jearold Winston. *Black Recreation: A Historical Perspective.* Chicago: Burnham/Rowman and Littlefield, 2002.

Holman, Gregory J. "It's Not a Boycott: NAACP Warns Nation About Traveling in Missouri." *Springfield News Leader* (July 30, 2017).

Hutchinson, Earl, Sr., with Earl Ofari Hutchinson. *A Colored Man's Journey Through 20th Century Segregated America.* Los Angeles, CA: Middle Passage Press Inc., 2000.

Ifill, Sherrilyn A. *On the Courthouse Lawn: Confronting the Legacy of Lynching in the Twenty-first Century.* Boston: Beacon Press, 2007.

Jackson, Algernon Brashear. *Jim and Mr. Eddy: A Dixie Motorlogue.* Washington, DC: Associated Publishers Inc., 1930.

Jackson, James A. "Big Business Wants Negro Dollars." *Crisis* (Feb. 1935): 45.

Jackson, Kenneth. *Crabgrass Frontier: The Suburbanization of the United States.* New York: Oxford University Press, 1985.

Jefferson, Alison Rose. "Lake Elsinore: A Southern California African American Resort Area During the Jim Crow Era, 1920s–1960s, and the Challenges of Historic Preservation Commemoration." MA thesis, Faculty of the School of Architecture University of Southern California, Los Angeles, Dec. 2007.

——. "Leisure's Race, Power, and Place: The Recreation and Remembrance of African Americans in the California Dream." PhD diss., University of California, Santa Barbara, Dec. 2015.

Jenkins, Carol, and Elizabeth Gardner Hines. *Black Titan: A. G. Gaston and the Making of a Black American Millionaire.* New York: Ballantine Books, 2004.

Johnson, Charles. *Patterns in Negro Segregation.* New York: Harper and Brothers, 1943.

Kahrl, Andrew William. "On the Beach: Race and Leisure in the Jim Crow South." PhD diss., Indiana University, Bloomington, May 2008.

King, Geoff. *Mapping Reality: An Exploration of Cultural Cartographies.* London: Macmillan, 1996.

Lauterbach, Preston. *The Chitlin' Circuit and the Road to Rock 'n' Roll.* New York: W. W. Norton, 2010.

Lawrence-Wehmiller, Paula. "Face to Face: Lessons Learned on the Teaching Journey." Friends Council on Education, 1992.

Lemann, Nicholas. *The Promised Land: The Great Black Migration and How It Changed America.* New York: Vintage Books, 1992.

Lewis, Tom. *Divided Highways: Building the Interstate Highways, Transforming American Life.* Ithaca, NY: Cornell University Press, 2013.

Life. "*Life* Visits Clifton's Cafeteria." (Nov. 27, 1944): 102–5.

Loewen, James W. *Sundown Towns: A Hidden Dimension of American Racism.* New York: New Press, 2005.

———. "Sundown Towns." *In Poverty & Race* (newsletter). Poverty and Race Research Action Council, 14, no. 6 (Nov.–Dec. 2005): 1–2, 6.

Los Angeles Sentinel. "Pearl Bailey Buys Murray's Desert Ranch." (June 23, 1955): A3.

Madigan, Tim. *The Burning: Massacre, Destruction, and the Tulsa Race Riot of 1921.* New York: St. Martin's Press, 2001.

Massey, Douglas S., and Nancy A. Denton. *American Apartheid: Segregation and the Making of the Underclass.* Cambridge, MA: Harvard University Press, 1998.

Mathewson, Tara Garcia. "How Poverty Changes the Brain." *Atlantic* (April 19, 2017).

McAlpin, Harry. "Army Abandons Plan for Jim-Crow Resort Centers." [Cleveland] *Call and Post* (Oct. 14, 1944): 1A.

———. "Army Abandons Plan to Segregate GI's." *Pittsburgh Courier* (Oct. 14, 1944): 1.

McWhorter, Diane. *Carry Me Home: Birmingham, Alabama: The Climactic Battle of the Civil Rights Revolution.* New York: Simon & Schuster, 2013.

Meier, August, and Elliot M. Rudwick. *From Plantation to Ghetto: An Interpretive History of American Negroes.* New York: Hill and Wang, 1966.

Morrison, Chic. "Happiness and Hope: Dedicated to Big Joe Rosenfield's Happiness Exchange and City of Hope." *New Pittsburgh Courier* (May 1962): 2.

Muhammad, Khalil Gibran. *The Condemnation of Blackness: Race, Crime, and the Making of the Modern Urban America*. Cambridge, MA: Harvard University Press, 2010.

Myrdal, Gunnar, and Sissela Bok. *An American Dilemma*. New York: Harper and Brothers, 1944.

New Pittsburgh Courier. "Breakthrough! Dealership Franchise Given Davis." (Nov. 1963): 18.

New York Amsterdam News. "Army Set to Take the Theresa." (Sept. 23, 1944): 1B.

———. "Green Book Points Way to Travellers." (1954): 46, 276.

———. "Services Held Victor Green." (Oct. 22, 1960): 4.

Norris, Frank. "Courageous Motorists: African American Pioneers on Route 66." *New Mexico Historical Review* 90, no. 3 (Summer 2015): 293–332.

Organized Kashruth Laboratories. *Kosher Food Guide* 6, no. 1. New York: Kosher Food Guide Publishers Inc., 1940.

Our World. "Negroes Spend Half a Billion Dollars on Cars a Year." (1955): 15–19.

Parker, Nancy. "Marsalis Mansion Owner Leaves a Legacy of Giving." Fox 8, Jan. 9, 2015.

Pell, Caliborne. "The Anthropological Differences Between Whites and Negroes." *Journal of Negro Education* 8, no. 4 (Oct. 1939): 688–93.

Pepin, Elizabeth. *Music of the Fillmore*, PBS.org. See www.pbs.org/kqed/fillmore/learning/music/swing.html.

Peyton, Thomas. *Quest for Dignity: An Autobiography of a Negro Doctor*. Los Angeles, CA, 1950.

Philadelphia Tribune. "Auto Salesman Awarded Chrysler-Plymouth Dealership." (Nov. 19, 1963): 5.

———. "Jim Crow Redistribution Policy Dropped by Army." (Oct. 7, 1944): 1.

Phillips, Kimberley L. *Daily Life During African American Migration*. Santa Barbara, CA: Greenwood Press, 2012.

Pittsburgh Courier. "Billy Butler to Publish Travel Guide." (May 8 1954): 18.

———. "Green Book in Its 26th Year." (June 1962): 19.

———. "Lindbergh and Lynching." (June 25, 1927): A8.

Ra-Shon Hall, Michael. "The negro traveller's guide to a Jim Crow South: negotiating racialized landscapes during a dark period in United States cultural history, 1936–1967." *Postcolonial Studies* 17, no. 3 (2014): 307–19.

Raitz, Karl. "American Roads, Roadside America." *Geographical Review* 88, no. 3 (1998): 363–87.

Ramsey, Calvin Alexander. *Ruth and the* Green Book. Minneapolis, MN: Carolrhoda Books, 2010.

Rapier, Arthur F. *Preface to Peasantry: A Tale of Two Black Belt Counties*. Columbia: University of South Carolina Press, 2005.

Roche, John P. "The Future of 'Separate but Equal.'" *Phylon* 12, no. 3 (3rd qtr., 1951): 219–26.

Rogers, Cleveland. "Robert Moses: An Atlantic Portrait." *Atlantic* (Feb. 1939).

Romeyn, Kathryn. "L.A.'s Ugly Jim Crow History: When Beaches Were Segregated." *Hollywood Reporter* (Aug. 5, 2016).

Rosenfield, Joe. *The Happiest Man in the World*. New York: Doubleday, 1955.

Rothstein, Richard. *The Color of Law: A Forgotten History of How Our Government Segregated America*. New York: W. W. Norton, 2017.

Rubio, Phillip F. *There's Always Work at the Post Office: African American Postal Workers and the Fight for Jobs, Justice, and the Economy*. Chapel Hill: University of North Carolina Press, 2010.

——. "Who Divided the Church? African American Postal Workers Fight Segregation in the Postal Unions, 1939–1962." *Journal of African American History* 94, no. 2 (2009): 172.

Rugh, Susan Sessions. *Are We There Yet? The Golden Age of American Family Vacations*. Lawrence: University Press of Kansas, 2008.

Sampson, Robert. *Great American City: Chicago and the Enduring Neighborhood Effect*. Chicago: University of Chicago Press, 2012.

Satter, Beryl. *Family Properties: How the Struggle Over Race and Real Estate Transformed Chicago and Urban America*. New York: Picador, 2010.

Seiler, Cotten. *Republic of Drivers: A Cultural History of Automobility*. Chicago: University of Chicago Press, 2008.

——. "'So That We as a Race Might Have Something Authentic to Travel By': African American Automobility and Cold-War Liberalism." *American Quarterly* 58, no. 4 (Dec. 2006): 1091–117.

Shumaker, Susan. "Untold Stories from America's National Parks: Segregation in the National Parks," PBS.org, 1:15–36. See www.pbs.org/nationalparks/media/pdfs /tnp-abi-untold-stories-pt-01-segregation.pdf.

Smith, Alfred K. "Army Backs Down on Theresa Hotel Seizure." *Chicago Defender* (Sept. 30, 1944): 5.

Smith, Craig. *Sing My Whole Life Long: Jenny Vincent's Life in Folk Music and Activism*. Albuquerque: University of New Mexico Press, 2007.

Stevenson, Bryan. *Just Mercy*. New York: Spiegel and Grau, 2015.

Sugrue, Thomas J. "Driving While Black: The Car and Race Relations in Modern America." *Automobile in American Life and Society* (Jan. 6, 2009).

——. *The Origins of the Urban Crisis: Race and Inequality in Postwar Detroit*. Princeton, NJ: Princeton University Press, 1996.

Sutton, H. "Negro Vacations: a Billion Dollar Business." *Negro Digest* 8 (July 1950): 25-27.

US News and World Report. "Push Is on for Mixed Pools and Parks." 52 (1962): 43-44.

U.S. Travel Bureau. *Negro Hotels and Guest Houses*. Washington, DC: U.S. Department of the Interior, 1941.

Van Deusen, John George. *The Black Man in White America*. Washington, DC: Associated Publishers, 1938.

Walker, Juliet E. K. *Encyclopedia of African American Business History*. Westport, CT: Greenwood Press, 1999.

——. *The History of Black Business in America: Capitalism, Race, and Entrepreneurship*. Chapel Hill: University of North Carolina Press, 2009.

Weems, Robert. *Desegregating the Dollar*. New York: New York University Press, 1998.

Weems, Robert E., and Lewis A. Randolph. "The Right Man: James A. Jackson and the Origins of the U.S. Government Interest in Black Business." *Enterprise and Society* 2, no. 2 (2005): 254-77.

Weyeneth, Robert R. "The Architecture of Racial Segregation: The Challenges of Preserving the Problematical Past." *Public Historian* 27, no. 4 (2005): 11-44.

Wilkerson, Isabel. *The Warmth of Other Suns*. New York: Vintage Books, 2011.

Wilson, Sondra K. *Meet Me at the Theresa: The Story of Harlem's Most Famous Hotel*. New York: Atria Books, 2004.

Wolcott, V. W. *Race, Riots, and Roller Coasters: The Struggle over Segregated Recreation in America*. Philadelphia: University of Pennsylvania Press, 2012.

Yee, Amanda. "Celebrating the African-American Shoebox Lunch." *Paste* (Feb. 21, 2017).

IMAGE CREDITS

Page vii: Courtesy of the Burford family. **Pages viii, xii, xiii, xviii, 2, 4, 14, 16, 38, 41, 45, 58-9, 64, 66, 68, 74, 80, 84, 85, 87, 93, 110, 123, 150, 157, 167, 178, 181, 182, 186, 188:** Victor H. Green & Co. **Page x:** Scurlock Studio Records, Archives Center, National Museum of American History, Smithsonian Institution. **Pages xvi, 10, 40, 43, 71, 73, 77, 78, 101, 103, 105, 112-13, 137, 143, 145, 154, 159, 169, 193, 204, 214, 220:** Photo by Author. **Page 9:** Courtesy of the Smithsonian National Museum of African American History and Culture. **Pages 12, 46:** Schomburg Center for Research in Black Culture, Photographs and Prints Division. **Page 13:** *New York Daily News* Archive/Getty Images. **Page 15:** Afro American Newspapers/Gado/Getty Images. **Pages 17, 49, 139:** Farm Security Administration, Office of War Information Photograph Collection, Library of Congress. **Page 21:** Richland Library, Columbia, SC. **Page 23:** Norman Transcript. **Page 25:** United States Patent Office, public domain. **Page 27:** Collection of the Smithsonian National Museum of African American History and Culture, gift of Dr. Teletia R. Taylor and descendants of Geraldine A. Taylor, proprietor, "Taylor's Playfair." **Page 28:** San Diego Air and Space Museum, Library and Archives. **Page 31:** Katherine G. Lederer Ozarks African American History Collection, Department of Special Collections and Archives, Missouri State University. **Page 33:** Byron Company/Museum of the City of New York. X2010.11.5170. **Pages 35, 48, 134:** Public domain. **Page 42:** *Washington Afro-American*. **Page 50:** Black History Collection, Manuscript Division, Library of Congress (024.00.00). **Page 52:** Bubley, Esther, photographer. Farm Security Administration, Office of War Information Photograph Collection, Library of Congress. **Page 55:** Arthur Siegel, Office of War Information, Harry S. Truman Library & Museum. **Page 57:** Vachon, John, photographer, Library of Congress Prints and Photographs Division, Washington, DC. **Page 62:** Robert K. Nelson, et al., "Mapping Inequality," *American Panorama*, ed. **Page 83:** Tichnor Brothers Collection. **Page 94:** WANN Radio Station

Image Credits

Records, Archives Center, National Museum of American History, Smithsonian Institution. **Page 96:** WANN Radio Station Records, Archives Center, National Museum of American History, Smithsonian Institution. **Page 98:** Robert Abbott Sengstacke/ Getty Images. **Page 106:** © Dr. Ernest C. Withers Sr., courtesy of the Withers Family Trust. **Pages 108, 114:** Courtesy of the Tom & Ethel Bradley Center at California State University, Northridge. **Page 117:** Hulton Archive/Getty Images. **Page 119:** Courtesy of Dino Thompson. **Page 125:** Mirro-Krome by H. S. Crocker. **Page 127:** Bolander's 5 & 10c Store, Cardcow. **Page 128:** "Doc" Helm Photography of Springfield, Illinois @1994. **Page 131:** Courtesy of Elizabeth Calvin. **Page 132:** Katherine G. Lederer Ozarks African American History Collection, Department of Special Collections and Archives, Missouri State University. **Page 135:** American National Red Cross Photograph Collection, Library of Congress. **Page 136:** Courtesy of the Threatt family. **Page 138:** American Stamp Company, Cardcow. **Page 148:** Collection of the Smithsonian National Museum of African American History and Culture, gift of Jackie Bryant Smith. **Page 163:** Fred Harvey Phostint. **Page 173:** *Detroit Free Press.* **Page 175:** Charles Moore/Getty Images. **Page 183:** Byron Company / Museum of the City of New York. X2010.11.5170. **Page 184:** Alabama Department of Archives and History. Donated by Alabama Media Group. Photo by Tom Self, *Birmingham News.* **Page 189:** Hulton Archive/Getty. **Pages 196, 197:** Courtesy of Kenneth Jackson. **Pages 198-99:** Bettmann/Getty Images. **Page 207:** AP/Shutterstock. **Page 209:** The Two-Way, NPR, August 3, 2017. **Page 217:** leezsnow/Getty Images. **Page 218:** Courtesy of Ron Burford.

INDEX

Note: Page numbers in *italics* refer to illustrations.

Index

Index

Index

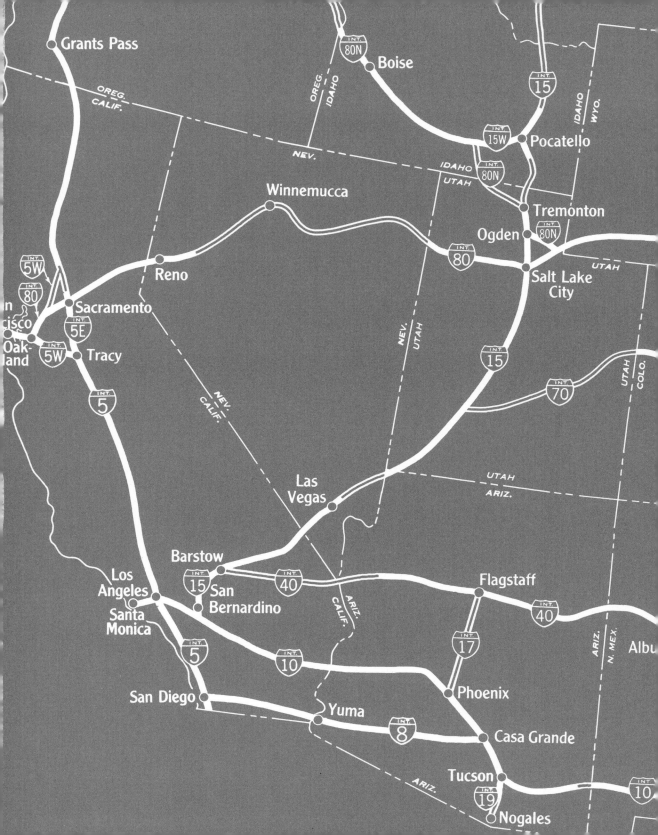

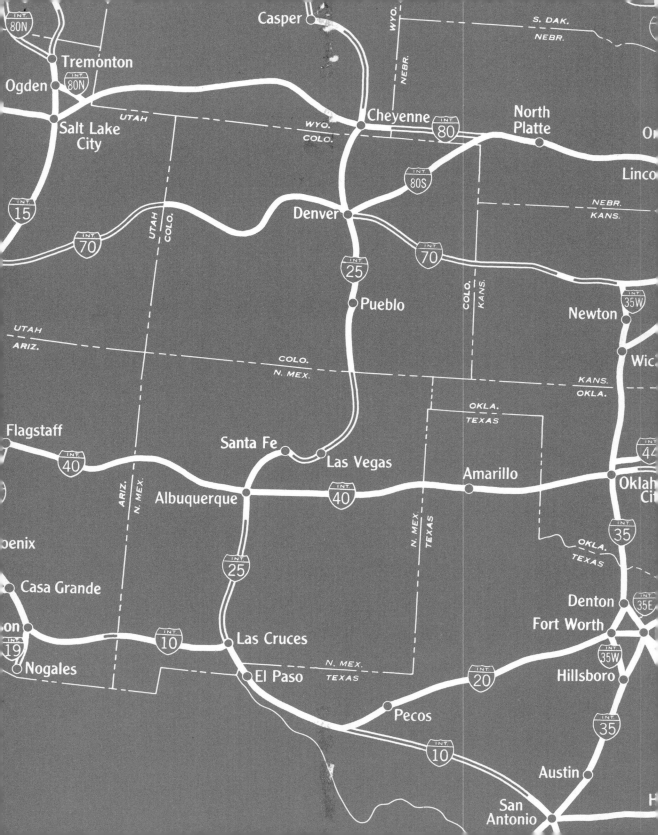